Paul O. Manz

The Enduring Legacy
of the Hymn Festival

James W. Freese

Lutheran University Press
Minneapolis, Minnesota

Paul O. Manz
The Enduring Legacy of the Hymn Festival
by James W. Freese

This monograph is adapted from a major document submitted on May 10, 2008, to the School of Music at Northwestern University, Evanston, Illinois, in partial fulfillment of the requirements for the degree, Doctor of Music (Program of Organ Performance).

Published under the auspices of:
Center for Church Music
Concordia University Chicago
River Forest, IL 60305-1499

ISBN-10: 1-932688-99-4

ISBN-13: 978-1-932688-99-3

Lutheran University Press
PO Box 390759
Minneapolis, MN 55439
Manufactured in the United States of America

Contents

Foreword

There is a group of organists and church musicians today who offer "Hymn Festivals." Being one of those, I'm often then asked the question: "What is a hymn festival?" Most often the assumption is that it is an informal gathering, where a number is called out, and everyone opens to that page and sings the hymn. Mention the name Paul Manz together with the description, and those who have experienced one of those famous events know immediately what they are. Not at all like an informal hymn sing.

We lucky ones who actually participated in Paul Manz's hymn festivals remember them vividly. They were an interesting juxtaposition of the known with the unexpected. We knew most of the hymns, but they were being sung in new creative ways we didn't know were possible, and the use of the organ was both evocative and enticing. These experiences, with the texts of the hymns and the vivid musical settings, went deep into the soul. Indeed, attending one of these events literally changed my life! As a young rock musician attending college to be a high-school choir teacher, I attended a Manz hymn festival and saw my two musical worlds come together: improvisation and singing, but with deep texts. I don't remember many of the songs my band played, but I remember the stanzas of "O God, Our Help in Ages Past" from that particular Paul Manz hymn festival.

By the end of his life-long calling, Paul Manz led perhaps thousands of assemblies in song using the form called "hymn festival" and through them revitalized the love of hymnody in the church, and freed up some rather limited uses of the organ. (Who else would combine a 32' reed with 1' flute for a melody illustrating something in the text?) Today there are several of us who offer "hymn festivals" on a regular basis, keeping these experiences alive.

But how did this program format develop?

James Freese unpacks Manz's life story as it related to the development of this unique form—stemming from recitals. They became cherished and highly anticipated events drawing capacity gatherings of eager singers around the world. Dr. Manz's experiences in life point to the work of the Holy Spirit—the experiences, contexts, and deep faith combining to give birth to this amazing gift to the Church. Dr. Manz's gifts were not limited to any one institution in his lifetime—and now we know, what he began is not limited to one generation. It lives on. It sings on.

Soli deo Gloria!

David Cherwien

Preface

The hymn festivals,[1] the attendant organ literature,[2] and the musical improvisations of Paul Manz have been enjoyed and discussed for decades. Scholarly research thus far[3] has covered detailed biographical data about Manz, some background on the hymn festivals, and an examination of Manz's compositional corpus, both organ and choral. None of it, to the author's knowledge, has had the hymn festival as its primary focus. This then was the impetus for the current study— to examine the origin of the Manz hymn festival and to trace the development of this genre from its beginnings.

Some biographical information necessary to show the development of Manz's requisite skills and awareness—both musically and theologically—is presented chronologically. The hymn festivals as entities are also traced chronologically, including explanations of the components of the festivals. Critical to an understanding of the genre, circumstances within the Church which affected Manz and the hymn festival are carefully delineated. In the final chapter, those lasting benefits which have become the legacy of the hymn festival are formulated and presented.

James W. Freese

Acknowledgments

I acknowledge with thanks those individuals who aided in bringing this paper to fruition: Paul and Ruth Manz, for their gracious hospitality during three unforgettable days together of interviewing; Dr. Charlotte Knoche, archivist at Concordia University—St. Paul, Minnesota, for providing copious amounts of photocopied hymn festival programs, always with a cheerful spirit; Rev. Dr. Mark Bangert, who provided archive materials from the Lutheran School of Theology in Chicago; Rev. Randall Lee, who opened his personal archives of the hymn festivals and provided valuable information; Dr. Carl Schalk, who provided useful information about the musical history at Grace Lutheran Church, River Forest, Illinois, and who first suggested the topic of this paper; Dr. Philip Gehring, who provided archival materials from Valparaiso University; Dr. David Cherwien who retrieved archival information from Mt. Olive Lutheran Church— Minneapolis, Minnesota; Concordia Historical Institute, for providing materials from the Lutheran Church–Missouri Synod's archives; Dr. Robert Harris, for his mentoring, meticulous proofreading, and insightful shaping of the manuscript; Prof. Margaret Kemper, for her constant encouragement; my colleagues at Concordia University Wisconsin, for their prayerful encouragement; and my dear wife, Jill, and children, Timothy and Lynn, who sacrificed greatly throughout the course of the doctorate, always affirming, caring, and loving.

Introduction

"Let the word of Christ dwell in you richly, as you teach and admonish one another in all wisdom, and as you sing psalms and hymns and spiritual songs with thankfulness in your hearts to God. And whatever you do, in word or deed, do everything in the name of the Lord Jesus, giving thanks to God the Father through him." So states the Apostle Paul in his letter to the Colossians (3:16-17). This passage could well serve as a maxim for the life and ministry of Paul Manz. The terms "life" and "ministry" intertwine when writing about Manz. To him they were one in the same. The author will use other significant Scriptural references to highlight this point. "Dwelling richly" also describes the fervor with which Manz approached the craft of leading congregational singing. In order to understand Manz's use of hymnody as a vehicle for his ministry, one must first understand the background of Lutheran hymnody and what part it played in Manz's early development.

The Lutheran Church has always been known as "the singing church." Martin Luther (1483-1546) gave the church's song back to the people in the form of the chorale. He did this so that the parishioners of his time could participate in the liturgy in the vernacular, singing the parts of the Mass entrusted to them. Luther saw hymn singing as a means of instruction in the basic tenets of the faith, as the song of royal priests, as proclamation as well as praise. His well-known statement about music being the "handmaiden of the Word" shows that the singing of hymns provides a carriage for the Gospel. Luther called it the "viva vox evangelii," the "living voice of the Gospel." "For Luther, music's chief function in worship as well as throughout the Christian life was, therefore, doxological proclamation: doxology or praise to the Creator, the 'God from whom all blessings flow,' and proclamation in grateful thanks for the redemption won for the world in Jesus Christ."[4] One cannot overstate these two elements—proclamation and praise—when speaking of the music ministry of Manz. Whereas Luther's contemporary, John Calvin (1509-64), was skittish about congregational song, limiting it to the unaccompanied unison singing of the Psalter, and his other contemporary, Ulrich Zwingli (1484-1531), eschewed congregational singing altogether (though he, himself, was a highly trained musician), Luther welcomed it with open arms. The hymn texts of the chorales found their way into the fabric of a family's life. Hymns that were sung at church were also sung and prayed at home. In his book, *Singing the Gospel: Lutheran Hymns and the Success of the Reformation*, Christopher Boyd Brown examines records of religious practices in the 16th- century Bohemian mining town of Joachimsthal in the wake of the Reformation. He notes,

> Just as burgher society expected its members to be competent amateur musicians, so too the Lutheran clergy expected their parishioners to be competent amateur theologians, able to apply God's Word to themselves and to their families in time of need. These two ideals were united in the institutions of the Lutheran Joachimsthal. In all of the town's pedagogical institutions—the schools, the church, *and especially the home* (emphasis the author's)—the Lutherans of Joachimsthal sought to take full advantage of the power of music to inculcate their religious message and to equip the laity of Joachimsthal with a knowledge of Lutheran doctrine sufficient to enable them to make a confession of their faith and to comfort themselves and others in time of need. The layman *in his home* (emphasis the author's) was both his own pastor and his own choir.[5]

As Lutheran immigrants came to the United States, they brought with them this emphasis on Christian song. It was into this rich tradition and understanding of hymnody that Paul Manz was born, raised, and nourished. Musical roots can be traced back to his paternal grandfather, who was the cantor of the local parish in Neudorf, Germany.[6] "All of Paul's nine uncles, with one exception, took turns at the organ of the parish."[7] By the age of nine, Manz was already playing organ for church services.

Paul Otto Manz was born May 10, 1919, in Cleveland, Ohio. He was the only child of Otto Heine Manz and Hulda Meta (née Jeske). "Both emigrated from a German settlement that is now behind the Polish frontier. On the paternal side, the Manz family had its roots in the area around Mainz in Germany, and 'Mainz' was in fact the original form of the family name."[8] Later, when the town came under Polish rule, their name was changed to "Malizewski." For some reason, saying "Paul Malizewski" does not roll off the tongue as readily as does "Paul Manz." Manz's "only child" status would factor into the decisions needed to be made as he went away to school.

Dr. Paul O. Manz

CHAPTER ONE

The Early Years

BOYHOOD

At an early age, Manz already showed great promise as a musician. By the time he was seven, he had "outgrown" his first piano teacher, Mrs. Dinda. She told his mother that she needed to get him another teacher because he had gone as far as she could take him. So, in the discussion, they decided to ask Henry Markworth, an organist in Cleveland, about lessons. Although all Manz wanted to do was play the organ, his grandfather thought it best that he first study piano.

Ruth Manz (Paul's wife) relates, "When he got to Henry Markworth, he said he would give Paul one organ lesson for every two piano lessons. When he got there in the morning, Henry was still getting ready, and his wife would give Paul milk and cookies. He ran you through a really strict theory background."[9]

Manz states, "First of all the piano literature. I had a good background from Mrs. Dinda. And then I studied the two-part and three-part inventions, some Bach, some Mozart, and some Beethoven. That was the first hour of my lessons. The second hour we would sit at the piano together, and he would give me a theme and say to play something on that."[10] (Improvisation was starting at age seven!) Ruth observed that there was the germ emerging of being able to improvise. "And then he told me about counterpoint. I never knew it; I didn't know how to spell it. We went through the species of counterpoint, believe it or not. I didn't know what it was at the time, but he was a very good teacher."[11]

THE RIVER FOREST YEARS (Prep School and College)

When Manz reached Concordia Teachers College in River Forest, Illinois (then a four-year high school and a four-year college) in 1933 as a fourteen-year-old high school freshman, he was about to embark upon a journey that would call for him to make many crucial decisions, overcome difficult obstacles, and receive an education that would propel him throughout his professional career. "My sainted mother would rather I had chosen theology—but music had chosen me—and this other—theology —was richly added to me."[12] This is much in the same way that Jesus said to His disciples, "Ye did not choose me, but I chose you, and appointed you, that ye should go and bear fruit, and that your fruit should abide: that whatsoever ye shall ask of the Father in my name, he may give it you" (John 15:16).

River Forest was a Lutheran Church–Missouri Synod institution that prepared men and women for the teaching ministry within the Synod. Long known for its fine music program, it also prepared classroom teachers to play hymns in the classroom and prepared students to be organists and choir directors. The religious training as well as the core curriculum was rigorous. Law and Gospel were taught to be rightly divided and applied both in teaching as well as disciplining and correct living. Religion was infused into the entire curriculum, and a devout faith was nourished by those who taught and cared for the students. Though misgivings crept to the surface in Manz's mind as well as those of his parents as they took leave of each other, they felt secure within an institution of *die liebe Synode,* (the dear Synod). One can but imagine Mr. and Mrs. Manz making their way back to Cleveland, which, for all intents and purposes, could have been a million miles away, without their dear Paul asking Papa in German after work as he often times did, "What have you brought me?" They sacrificed greatly, and would be called upon to sacrifice to an even greater measure to give their son the best education and avenue to be a church musician.

One of the first challenges Manz faced was not being allowed to take organ while in high school, as that right was reserved for those in college. Manz had already been playing for services since he was nine years old. In his first organ recital in Cleveland at the age of 14, he played Henri Mulet's (1878-1967) *Carillon Sortie,* a piece often taught to graduate students, and a piece he would quote in one of his latest improvisations, "We, Who Once Were Dead"(Tune: MIDDEN IN DE DOOD).[13] He felt surely he would be allowed to study organ; however, this was not the case.

"Instead, he was forced back to piano under Richard T. Rohlfing. While he did not appreciate this at first, Manz later regarded this as a blessing in disguise since it opened up for him new musical literature, principally the romantic composers such as Grieg and Chopin. He loved it. As a climax to this career on the piano, he was asked to play the Schumann concerto with the college band."[14]

When Manz finally became a college student, his eager anticipation of studying organ was again dashed. He found out his instruction would not be private lessons, but group lessons with three other students. Ironically, Manz, the student with the most talent and promise, was given the smallest portion of the lesson— ten minutes out of fifty— because the other students needed more help. This exasperation led to a phone call home and a decision to seek private organ instruction elsewhere. River Forest's proximity to Chicago gave Manz ample choices of places to study. He decided to study with Edwin Eigenschenk at the American Conservatory in Chicago. For two years he carried on this arrangement without the knowledge of the instructors at Concordia. It is just as well they did not know. Manz's organ professor at River Forest, Martin Lochner, (1883-1945), also happened to be a pupil of Eigenschenk at the very same time.

Manz had already felt the wrath of Lochner when he played for chapel at River Forest. Lochner was the organist at Grace Lutheran Church, a Missouri Synod congregation situated on the northeast corner of Concordia's campus, and a "training school" for those who wanted to be teachers. Lochner had been the congregation's organist since 1919, thirteen years before Grace's relocation to that site from its previous location. He was also was the author of *The Organist's Handbook: A Guide to Lutheran Service Playing on Small Pipe-Organ, Reed-Organ, or Piano* (CPH, 1940). In it he stated that,

"Congregational singing is *Volkgesang*, and the chorales and hymns must therefore be played in their simple form, usually as they are given in the *Choralbuch* and hymn-book, but adapted to your instrument." In other words, "Play what is written!" He went on to write, "Stops must therefore not be changed too frequently, 'word-painting' must not be resorted to, sudden changes from loud to soft must be avoided—all of which bewilders the singers."

Manz felt he had developed a good background for harmonizations as a Concordia student. "In fact, I would play for chapel in the old chapel (known on campus as the *aula*) upstairs, and I remember once the first time I got chewed out terribly by Martin Lochner. 'You didn't play what was written!' And later I was playing again—I didn't play that often for chapel, because all the organists that were going to be teachers had to play for chapel—perhaps once every three months. He really chewed me out again. 'You have to play exactly what's written, nothing more and nothing less!' And I have to say this: I had complete freedom in my own mind how to harmonize that hymn. I watched the harmonic rules. They were instinctive in my memory. But they were different, and that is what Lochner was objecting to."[15]

After two years of this duplicitous situation, Lochner learned that he and Manz shared the same organ professor. Lochner took this matter to the faculty and complained bitterly to the extent that Manz was prohibited from taking any more lessons or practicing at Concordia. Concordia's most promising student, who one day would become its most famous church musician, had to continue his training outside the "friendly" confines of Concordia. (Later in life, Manz and Lochner mended their differences and developed a cordial relationship.) This was a blessing in disguise. Eigenschenk was an excellent organist, and also took a liking to Manz. He reduced his usual $5 lesson fee to $3 (even three dollars was a princely sum at that time). "My parents made it possible for me to go to the American Conservatory of Music. My mother sold Sunshine Christmas greeting cards."[16]

Often times the lesson was followed by dinner together, since Manz would have arrived back on campus after the dining hall had closed.[17] "Under this eminent tutor, romantic organ literature, largely French, became a reality: Dupré, Seth Bingham, Guilmant, Gigout, and Vierne. Such literature was excellent preparation for his later study with Flor Peeters."[18]

To be sure, Eigenschenk was a taskmaster. "The first thing Eigenschenk did when I came for a lesson in Kimmel Hall, he said, 'Take off your belt.' I thought, 'What is going on here?' He strapped my legs and said, 'Now, play.' He was French-trained with [Joseph] Bonnet (1884-1944). And then when I played he hit my hand. 'Don't move your hand!' He played a recital at Grace Church. Lochner (his *other* pupil) had him play there. There was no movement in his body. Not a thing going on. But what music he produced! He put an empty water glass on my hands. 'Don't break that glass. Now play!' His was a shock method."[19]

In summers during his River Forest days, Manz studied with Edwin Arthur Kraft (1883-1962) in Cleveland. Manz's parents made it possible for him to do that as well (Appendix 1, p.73).

He was at Trinity Cathedral. He had a huge, huge Skinner organ. He arranged many of the classic organ pieces like the preludes by Liszt and other pieces and had them published by G. Schirmer. And in the rear of the church he had them dig a hole to the left of the nave about twelve feet deep and six feet this way and three feet this way. He had Skinner put in three tubas: two 8' stops, a 4', and a 16' all on high pressure. Once or twice a year, but certainly on Easter day, he would play the "Ride of the Walküre." And when he opened up those tubas, those old ladies just flew out of their seats. I think it was at my last lesson I said to him in German, "*Ich habe eine Bitte.*" "What is that?" "Ride of the Valkyries." And I went back there and he played it. You have never heard such a magnificent sound in that cathedral when he let loose with those tuba mirables. He could play up a storm and was a magnificent sight reader. Whatever I played for him for a lesson I chose what I played myself. I wanted to get his thoughts on other things. He would always give me something else. When I left he would say, "For next week I want you to play this: all three movements of a Guy Weitz symphony." An Englishman (1883-1970). Notes all over the page. "That's your lesson." That was a good experience. And even during the lesson—if he didn't give me something to take home with me because the lesson ran too long or too short he would say, "Here, now play this." He taught me to sight read. [20]

During the summer of 1941, immediately upon graduating from River Forest, Manz seized yet another opportunity to study with another notable organist and Bach scholar, Albert Riemenschneider (1878-1950). Riemenschneider had founded the Baldwin Wallace Conservatory of Music in Berea, Ohio, in 1899. It would become one of the most important sites for Bach research in the United States. The Bach Riemenschneider Institute, as listed on their web site, is the "guardian of priceless Bach-related manuscripts and first editions."[21] Manz studied Bach exclusively with Riemenschneider every week during that summer. At the end of the summer, Riemenschneider invited Manz into his study and let him actually handle the Bach manuscripts. What an education within an education for such a young man about to embark on a career of making church music!

CHAPTER TWO

Professional Experiences and Advanced Study

MT. OLIVE LUTHERAN CHURCH—MINNEAPOLIS, MINNESOTA

One would think that great inspiration for organ improvisations and stirring hymn playing would come from a magnificent instrument. Such was not the case at Mt. Olive, the church Manz came to in 1946. Its organ was anything but stellar. The Welte-Tripp organ, installed in 1931 when Mt. Olive was built, was a unified, romantic-sounding instrument with no upperwork, save the super couplers. Manz characterized the relationship between Welte and Tripp as one where Welte was a millionaire, and Tripp knew something about organ building. He believes it was one of the last organs that they built. (There is a large Welte-Tripp organ in the Shove Chapel of Colorado College. It was *the* last one built, also in 1931, and portions of it are still there, although it has subsequently been rebuilt.) While it would have suited itself well to the music of Mendelssohn and perhaps even Franck, it didn't come close to the sound associated with the improvisations and hymn playing of Manz (Appendix 2, pp. 74-75). Nonetheless, Manz drew praise for his "overcoming" the deficiencies of the instrument. A review by D. Byron Arneson (a member of the American Guild of Organists, now living in Greensboro, North Carolina) of the October 28, 1951, organ concert by Manz stated the following:

> For a program of organ music revealing technique, color contrast, excellent rhythm and musical imagination, hear a Paul Manz recital! Mr. Manz seems to display all these qualities in ever-increasing amounts in each of his organ

recitals. His ability to worm so much effective dynamic and coloristic contrasts, including some sparkling "baroque" registrations, and so many seemingly brilliant and thunderous climaxes out of an organ almost hopelessly bogged down with obese Phonon Diapasons and lethargic Trombas is simply uncanny.

He showed this ability to the utmost in the Hindemith *Second Sonata* and again at the end of the program when he left the keys smoking after Bach's *Fugue a la Gigue* [*sic*], playing with terrifying speed and accuracy.

Also noticeable is the sensitiveness and feeling for beauty which Mr. Manz exhibits in the more intimate compositions. Particularly expressive was his second of three Bach transcriptions, *Have Mercy upon Me.*

Special mention must be made of Mr. Manz's convincing rhythm, his controlled use of rubato, and his smooth retards. One could ask for no greater perfection here. Mr. Manz likewise can play a beautiful worship service, as the opening and closing hymn accompaniments and vesper liturgy revealed. Let us look forward with eagerness to future recitals by this very talented artist.[22]

Manz dutifully labored to the best of his abilities with the instrument from 1946 until July 1952, when some long-overdue rebuilding was undertaken and completed on the organ by Harry O. Iverson of Minneapolis, the local Möller Organ Company representative. The firm of John Gould and Sons of St. Paul worked under the supervision of Mr. Iverson (Appendix 3, pp. 77-79). The rebuild gave the organ more upperwork and color. It was not until 1966 that the Schlicker organ was installed at Mt. Olive (Appendix 4, p. 80). Manz waited a full 20 years to have an organ of the caliber he would become accustomed to playing in Belgium, Germany, and around the United States and beyond as a recitalist and leader of hymn festivals.

Manz's "solemn call" (appointment) to Mt. Olive was as Minister of Music and Christian Education. As such he directed both adult and children's choirs and played for services. The balcony at Mt.

Olive became fertile ground for Manz as he honed his skill at both repertoire and service playing. Paramount within the service was the playing of the hymns and the hymn introductions—improvisations—which prepared the parishioners for the hymn about to be sung. In improvisation lessons with Manz, the author was taught that the improvisation or introduction was to serve three purposes: to announce the hymn tune, to set the tempo, and to set the mood of the hymn's text.

During his early years at Mt. Olive, Manz studied with Arthur B. Jennings at the University of Minnesota and Pilgrim Congregational Church in Minneapolis. "He was an excellent teacher, and I learned many things from him—style, registration, fingering and hymn accompaniments. Years later I became his legal guardian for the last years of his life."[23] Manz stated that Jennings was the most influential person in the way he played hymns. "He had an entirely different approach to hymn playing than I was accustomed to. I was used to just playing the hymn and be done with it. I heard Jennings play hymns and that was just mind-boggling."[24] Manz reflected on the state of church music during that time. "In the '40s, the tenor of church music was largely sweet. For the most part, choral music was limited to anthems, the organ was turgid, lacked luster, and creative leadership was minimal. Church music was in a stagnant state. The apex of the service was the homily, and the Eucharist was offered four times a year."[25] He further stated, "Hymn singing at that time was perfunctory, and he [Jennings] tried to liven it up by playing lush harmonies, which he did. And his congregation lovingly responded. His registrations tended to be rather on the lush side because of the organ he had (a 4-manual Skinner)."[26]

Manz later studied with Flor Peeters in Belgium in 1955, and was reluctant to play a recital when he returned to Minneapolis. His work with Flor Peeters had brought about a distinct change in style from what Jennings had taught him, and because of this, he was reluctant for fear of offending his mentor. Eventually he did perform and Jennings did take notice of the style change. While there was some apprehension on Jennings' part, he respected the style change that had taken place. That mutual admiration was shown in the later stages of Jennings' life was indicative of the fact that Manz was appointed Jennings' legal guardian, and for a time Jennings lived with the Manzes, who were his caregivers. One of Manz's most frequently played works, "Jesus, Lead Thou On" in *The Parish Organist* series is dedicated to Jennings. Knowing the text of this hymn (Appendix 5, p. 81) and the quiet beauty of the setting, one can see why Manz chose to dedicate this piece to "Herr" as he was affectionately known.[27]

CONCORDIA COLLEGE—ST. PAUL, MINNESOTA

When Manz received the divine call to Concordia College, St. Paul, Minnesota, in 1957 to be a professor of music, he was told that one of the stipulations of the call was that he was to relinquish his duties as Minister of Music at Mt. Olive. He immediately returned (declined) the call, much to the puzzlement of the college. Manz told them that his position at Mt. Olive was the embodiment and realization of all his teaching about church music. It was *here* at Mt. Olive where he put his ideas into practice. Without such a "laboratory" or sounding board for his ideas as a practicing church musician, his teaching would ring hollow.[28] It is improbable to think an individual would turn down a call to a synodical college. Manz's case was obviously well made, in that the college immediately re-issued the call with the provision that he could retain his position at Mt. Olive. He, did, however, relinquish his duties as Minister of Christian Education.

FULBRIGHT SCHOLAR—STUDY WITH FLOR PEETERS

As previously mentioned, Manz's skills were honed by one of the greatest living organists of the 20th century, the Belgian, Flor Peeters (1903-1986). In 1955 Manz was awarded a Fulbright scholarship to study for a year with Peeters in Antwerp, Belgium, at the Royal Flemish Conservatory of Music where Peeters was organ instructor. Peeters was also titular organist of the Cathedral of Saint Rombout in Mechelen, Belgium. Such a prestigious grant also held bright promise for the Manz family, since the entire family would move to Belgium for Manz's year of studies. Manz states, however, "The Lutheran community of the church was not at all supportive when in 1955 I went to Belgium to study with Flor Peeters who was Roman Catholic—because they said there were any number of good

Lutheran organists in Germany with whom I ought to associate."[29] Despite such rumblings, Manz forged ahead.

Peeters represented a strong link in the French Romantic organ heritage, having studied with Charles Tournemire (1870-1939), a pupil of César Franck (1822-1890). Tournemire, Franck's successor once removed as organist at Ste. Clothilde in Paris, held that post for over forty years.[30] The close relationship between Tournemire and Peeters can be seen in the disposition of the original organ console of Ste. Clothilde on which Franck played. A priceless possession, the console had been willed to Peeters by Tournemire's widow and brought to Peeters' home by U.S military troops in a Jeep at the request of Peeters. It was then situated in his living room (Appendix 6, p. 82).

In his study with Peeters, Manz's harmonic vocabulary was about to be greatly expanded as was his understanding of French Romantic organ registration. He was also about to enter a crucible of performance pressure that would later pay rich dividends as he was frequently requested to perform hymn festivals in many locations in which he was always presented with a new set of circumstances and challenges. Although Manz had his mind set on what he wanted to study, his ideas, however, would soon be subordinated to those of Peeters.

When Manz went to study with Peeters, he wanted to study the organ works of Bach. When the Manz family first met his teacher on the steps of the cathedral, he was told he would be studying the "Alte Nederlands Meisters" (Old Netherlands Masters). Ruth (Paul's wife) looked at him in disbelief and said, "No!" Peeters said, "Ja!" Peeters held sway. Manz recalls,

> He started me out with people I had never heard of. He knew them inside out. They were in his genes. He wrote a three-volume book of music from the Old Dutch Meisters and chose the best music they ever wrote, and his students had to play some of those *things*. I didn't have to play all of them because I already had a background. But the first-year students had to go to all the classes. We went to class together and heard four of his

best organists. We didn't get to play, not with Flor. There were anywhere between eighteen and twenty students in the class, and you listened to the Bach "Prelude and Fugue in A Minor" with this [*sic*] student, and after that you would listen to the Bach "Fantasy and Fugue in G Minor" with all the students. You learned how to phrase and play what was his style. So when you got to the top of the line and *you* were the one who played, the others sat back to listen, and you were expected to play in that style and with that interpretation.[31]

The first time Manz went to class, he ran out of gas on the way, arriving late with quite a stench of gasoline on him from an emergency fill up. He was mortified to make his first appearance in such a condition. His first assignment was to watch.

First of all we sat in the auditorium, all twenty of us, and I didn't see Flor. I had met him. I went over to his house with my family to introduce ourselves. All of a sudden the door opened up and he walked in, and all the students just rose. I rose with them. I was as nervous as a kitten. I was actually going to go to this class. So he said to the first one, "You play!" As soon as he got on the bench everyone would gather around the console. While the student was playing the piece, if a student didn't like a certain stop tab, he would shut it off or change it to something else. Can you imagine? I was just *trembling* in my boots. They had pages to turn. Someone would deign to turn pages for him. I wondered what would happen when *I* got up there. He spoke only Flemish. That did not bother me that much because there is a commonality between Flemish and German and, subsequently, English. Some words are the same. I didn't always understand the verbs.

After he had his four people play—and each played about 30-45 minutes—he would ask the students what they heard. The students would make polite comments, and Peeters would say to the student, "Do you agree with that?" The student could defend himself. And then

Peeters would sum it up and say what was wrong here, what was good here, and what had to be improved. "I didn't like what you did here. Watch it next time."

Then, he finally said—and I'll say it in English, although he said it in Flemish, and I knew what he was saying—"Now we have a student just coming here for the first time. He is an Americaner. He will play for us—a Lutheran organist and choir director." I could hear the comments, "Ooh, who is that?" I could just see the response. "He will play. What will you play, Paul?" I chose two movements of the *Symphony No. 4* by Widor, which I played from memory. Normally, as I mentioned earlier, the students would change registrations if they didn't like them, but they wouldn't *dare* come up to the console when I was playing because Flor just gave them a look and that stopped them. The five of us were friendly. One of them left, so there were only four left.[32]

Manz also had a three-hour private lesson with Peeters every week. During that time he learned to improvise in the French tradition. It is noteworthy that such a skill was also a given requirement for all organists studying not only with Peeters in Belgium, but also at the Paris Conservatoire or elsewhere in France. Improvisation on a given theme continues to be a standard part of a French recital. Such skills served Manz well in his own improvisations—a combination of technique and knowledge. (Note: The regimen of improvisation was *the* major component of the lessons the author had with Manz. The music rack was *always* empty during the lessons.)

Peeters encouraged Manz to vie for the first prize in organ and improvisation along with the other three students. "The day of the contest we were sequestered in four different rooms to sit there and dwell on our sins and shudder in our boots," Manz recalled. Ruth Manz added, "Because the judges were out there waiting to devour you."[33] Paul continued:

There were five judges from the other conservatories throughout Belgium. In May we had the prelims, and I had to play something from each period: early Flemish, late Flemish, baroque, romantic, and contemporary. I would be able to play one piece flawlessly. Each of us had to do that. If you made one mistake in the prelims, they had a cowbell, and they'd ring it. That was it. Try it again next year. For that prelim we had to play the same phrasing for each piece. If three did and one did not, he was out. After that we were told we all made it. We were not given any grades. That meant that we were eligible for the final. One month later we came back, and we played one piece of a contemporary nature and one major Bach piece—that was it. I played the Bach "Fantasy and Fugue in G Minor," a Franck piece, and the "Variations on an Old Flemish Carol" by Flor Peeters. It was a stunning piece.

In June we came back and competed against each other. That was tough because we were friends. The others had studied as much as three or four years for this moment, and this was my first and only year from America. Everyone's family was there cheering. I played third or fourth. Afterward there was a sigh of relief, I was so nervous.

Later we (all the families and contestants) met in a beautiful garden. The judges finally appeared. We were offered something to eat, but I don't think I ate anything. I don't think I could. The announcement was made: I had won the first prize with distinction![34]

Manz, along with the other students, also took composition lessons with Peeters once a month, which sometimes lasted four hours or more. Paul recalled:

Four people were in the class. He would make an assignment. The composition would be played a month later for the class. Notably once I wrote a piece using four psalms as a background. Peeters would sit down and play these. His class of twenty or more organ students liked these. He would ask, 'What did you hear?' The class would tear them apart. Then Flor would give his comments. They would listen to you and then after it was over they would make more comments. "Well, there were parallel fifths or an unresolved seventh in a measure." Then you would have to answer. So you defended yourself and said that I did it that way because that was exactly how I felt at the time.[35]

One time Manz, then 35 years old, pulled out one of Peeters' Op. 69 preludes in response to what Peeters had told Manz about one of his compositions. Manz showed Peeters a parallel fifth in the piece in front of the entire class. Peeters calmly said, "Oh, that's okay because I did it."[36]

Peeters' Op. 69 chorale preludes were but one of over thirty volumes of chorale preludes he composed despite the fact that the Catholic Church did not sing hymns at that time. Manz regards Peeters' Op. 68, 69, and 70 to be some of his finest chorale preludes of the genre. In these works, which Manz said all students should study, Peeters demonstrates a wide treatment of the chorales. The author finds it amazing that, according to Manz, Peeters *never* composed at a keyboard, but rather always wrote in his study. This is a completely different way of composition for chorale preludes from that of Manz who wrote at the organ; yet some of the language of Peeters, particularly in the use of ritornellos, is found in Manz's music. After his year of study was completed, Manz returned to Belgium for three additional summers to work with Peeters in composition, organ, and improvisation.[37]

FULBRIGHT SCHOLAR—
STUDY WITH HELMUT WALCHA

Because of his accomplishments, Manz's Fulbright scholarship was extended, but Paul had to return to the United States and his responsibilities. He did, however, agree to use the next summer for study with Helmut Walcha (1907-1991) at the Hochschule für Musik in Frankfurt, Germany. Walcha, though blind, was considered to be one of the greatest living German organists. He had learned the entire works of Bach by rote. After having someone play a line of a piece for him, he would play it back. Line by line, measure by measure, phrase by phrase, the complete works of Bach were learned in this fashion.

Walcha's three volumes of *Choralvorspiele* (chorale preludes), which demonstrate a wide range of compositional techniques and rich and varied registrations, were very influential to a very receptive and impressionable Manz. The fact that Manz spoke fluent German helped in developing a rapport and relationship with Walcha. As with Riemenschneider, Manz learned Baroque music, primarily Bach, on instruments that had radically different stop lists from those in Belgium. When the author asked about the disposition of the organ at Dreikönigskirche in Frankfurt, Manz replied that the only string stop on the organ was perhaps a Geigen. Unlike the French Romantic organs in Belgium, replete with the warm, orchestral sounds associated with Franck and that school of music, the organ at Walcha's church was very much in the style of the *Werkprinzip* (*Werk* principle), "completeness of each division and contrast between divisions, placement of divisions, and their architectural appearance"[38] (Appendix 7, p. 82). It is probable that the disposition of the organ did lend itself to registration suggestions within Manz's published preludes and the registrations used at hymn festivals for improvisations. During a lesson with Manz, the author was told that the organ has many colors. Use them!

Walcha did not teach improvisation to Manz, but he did improvise within the service. In his "Notes on Interpretation" in Volume II of his preludes, Walcha gives his rationale for writing these pieces. Though Walcha did not teach improvisation *per se*, he did model it and put it in the context of hymn singing and worship.

> These chorale preludes, like the first collection, are addressed to the Christian congregation, offering instrumental elaboration on the *texts* and *tunes* of hymns [emphasis mine]. Regular and unceasingly varied chorale prelude improvisations, as required by the Lutheran worship which I have served for several decades, forms [*sic*] their background. While suited for use in much of the organist's practical work, they are conceived for performance *right before the hymn, to stimulate and enliven subsequent singing* [emphasis mine].[39]

Manz recalls,

> I attended a number of his services to hear him play at his church. I remember one particular time I met him and said that I would see him in church. When I met him at the door he took my arm, and on the way up to the balcony he said to me in German, "What is the hymn for today?" I told him and he said, "Oh, ja!" That was the first time he knew what hymn he was going to play, and he would improvise on it, but not as a prelude to the hymn. At the end there was always a *Nachspiel* (postlude), so he didn't know what the hymn was until I told him. There was one hymn in the 5:00 Saturday service. That was the hymn on which he improvised at the end of the *Gottesdienst* (Divine Service). His intonation of the hymn was decorated, but nothing extraordinary. The big improvisation came at the end, and people sat for that. They were trained to do that. He was good for his time. Walcha was perhaps the best organist in Germany, although some thought Karl Richter was.[40]

One anecdote recounted by Manz highlights the genius of Walcha. During a lesson with Walcha in the balcony of Walcha's church, Manz was playing a Bach prelude. At a certain point Walcha would find his way to the console and turn the page at the wrong time. Not wanting to embarrass Walcha, Manz turned back to the correct page and continued. This happened a number of times within the piece, much to Manz's consternation. Afterward Manz delicately broached the subject, mentioning to Walcha that he had turned the pages at the wrong place. Walcha asked Manz what edition of Bach he was using. When Manz told him, Walcha replied that he was turning pages according to a different edition. He had memorized all the page turns.[41]

CHAPTER 3

The Hymn Festivals

THE GENESIS OF THE HYMN FESTIVAL

One would think that Paul Manz was always known as an improvisor and a leader of stirring hymn festivals. Quite the opposite is true. The hymn festivals at Mt. Olive actually began as organ recitals. Manz recalled,

> It all started not with a hymn festival but with organ recitals. I would always plan to have an organ recital in fall at Mt. Olive. After about the second one always once a year, I decided to open up with a hymn and close with a hymn, and there were enough people there to make it worthwhile. So a hymn started the organ recital and a hymn closed it. Well, there was such a spontaneous response to the hymns that after a number of years I decided, hey, I'm going to do a festival of hymns or something, and that caught on like wildfire because people loved to sing. The church was getting gradually fuller and fuller every time I did that to the point where about the third or fourth year we would announce an organ recital and it was really was a hymn, hymn, hymn, maybe some organ pieces, and a hymn and, the people just ate up those hymns like mad. They loved to sing. And I thought to myself, let's just do a hymn festival, so it was really biting the bullet, and I didn't know it would continue, but it did. The church was packed. In fact, after a couple of years, an hour before the doors were opened the church was beginning to get full. People were in line. It was amazing. They just loved to sing.[42]

Archival material and his personal recollection were not able to pinpoint the exact year of the first hymn festival. It is known from archival material that annual organ recitals did continue at Mt. Olive until 1964.

When asked about the statement made by some that he conceived the idea of a hymn festival while attending Northwestern University, Manz responded,

> I went to Northwestern for a summer session, a two-week summer session. They gave me credit for it later when I went for my master's. They had a man, the secretary of the American Hymn Society, I don't remember his name. One of the items on the list was to sing hymns. And this was my first experience with the so-called hymn festival.
>
> But, what that amounted to was, "Let's do Hymn 23, the first one." If there were five stanzas, we might do three. "And then let's do Hymn 56." That was my first concept of a program of hymns. It was a hymn sing. The place— Lutkin Hall— was packed because it was a conference going on, and I was a part of the conference. So this is how the idea germinated in my brain subconsciously. I think this was after Europe.[43]

Ruth Manz agreed, adding, "I remember you were always being very sensitive about doing even a recital. At first because you were concerned about how it would affect Arthur Jennings, because it was a departure from what you had been taught before. So then you started doing more hymns."[44]

Manz added, "I appreciated and learned a great deal from Arthur Jennings' style of hymn playing, which I tried to emulate, because I was so impressed with it, and he really knew how to get the congregation to sing. (Jennings was at Plymouth Congregational Church in Minneapolis in addition to his duties as Professor or Music at the University of Minnesota). He used very lush harmonies. He had a big Aeolian Skinner organ, and he could do that. He had the material. I didn't have the material (instrument), but [I tried to do it] through touch, through legato, through staccato, and hopefully through imaginative improvs at Mt. Olive."[45]

Returning to the subject of Mt. Olive hymn festivals, Manz said, "I wouldn't play a postlude. I played a prelude and then went right into the festival, and the people took to it like a duck takes to water. People loved to sing, and the AGO (American Guild of Organists) supported it very well."

Ruth added, "Yes, you played literature. The offering was a place for the literature. The literature was 'in, with, and under' the hymn festival." [46]

Questioned whether narrations were used between the hymns in the early days, Ruth recalled that they were provided by Reverend (Alton) Wedel, pastor of Mt. Olive. Some were biblical selections. Then later, Pastor Wedel wrote and collected them. They were very apropos. One collection from which Wedel read was entitled *A Bag of Noodles*[47] (Appendix 8, p. 83), at the time a very "modern sounding" collection from the late sixties and early seventies. They stand in marked contrast to the profound readings used in later hymn festivals.

When asked about his faith-based rationale for holding hymn festivals, in other words, for more than purely musical reasons, Manz replied, "I did it for musical reasons, but I used Scripture and related readings to highlight the hymns and music improvisations and prayers. That is all I can say. I think my faith came through in the playing and choice of hymns." Ruth added that she didn't think he ever consciously sat down and defined it. [48]

THE READINGS

One of the most meaningful components of the hymn festivals was the attendant reading that preceded each of the hymns. A person at the host congregation, oftentimes the pastor, was charged with finding readings that would prepare the listener to understand further the text of the hymn that was about to be sung. Though only a portion of the readings have been preserved, they show that much thought was poured into finding just the right reading to match the theological content of the hymn text. Although Manz did not screen them beforehand, the readings at the many hymn festivals kindled a fresh awareness preceding the playing of the hymn. The profundity of thought, prose, poetry, and Scripture paired with the hymn made for emotionally charged hymn singing. The writings of several noted theologians and writers, among whom were Martin Luther, Martin Franzmann, John Wesley, Dietrich Bonhöffer, O.P. Kretzmann, William Shakespeare, Søren Kierkegaard, Martin Marty, and Christina Rosetti were read. One of the more emotional readings, written by Dr. Martin Marty and read by him at a hymn festival at The Evangelical Lutheran Church of St. Luke in Chicago, Illinois, November 14, 1999, preceded the hymn "Lord, Thee I Love with All My Heart."

We know that someday there will be a last event for each of us in this room. Married couples know something that never gets voiced at weddings, that some day one of the two will fold the eyelids of the other. Parents have to weep at the death and burial of children. Yet such awarenesses inspire not morbidity, but only seriousness, because the God of the future goes before us and God's presence is there.

I have a gloss on the key line of the first verse where we sing, "Yea, heaven itself were void and bare If Thou, Lord, wert not near me." I associate with a story from the legends that go with Bernard of Clairvaux. A man was confronted by an angel who bore a pitcher of water and a torch. Why? The angel answered, "To quench the fires of hell and burn the pleasures of heaven so that people will start loving God, not out of fear or selfish desire, but for God's own sake."

The chorale speaks for all of us when it says, "And should my heart for sorrow break." Some losses, some discoveries, some separations, some alienations, some inner weaknesses are so profound, that they do lead to hearts breaking for sorrow. Think about what rends and what breaks your own heart, and then sing, "My trust in Thee can nothing shake." Thus, the chorale prepares us for a life in the love of God, not in a void and bare heaven, but in a full and rich here and now, there and then.[49]

This prepared the congregation for the singing of the hymn with special emphasis on the last stanza, which took the singers from the closed coffin in the grave all the way to heaven and the eternal song of the Lamb in his kingdom.

> Lord, let at last Thine angels come,
> To Abr'ham's bosom bear me home,
> That I may die unfearing;
> And in its narrow chamber keep
> My body safe in peaceful sleep
> Until thy reappearing.
> And then from death awaken me,
> That these mine eyes with joy may see,
> O Son of God, thy glorious face,
> My Savior and my fount of grace.
> Lord Jesus Christ,
> My prayer attend, my prayer attend,
> And I will praise thee without end![50]

THE DEVELOPMENT OF THE HYMN CORPUS

Each individual hymn festival used one set of hymns developed around a theme, whether of the church year or a particular season of the church year such as Easter or Reformation. The hymns for a specific hymn festival were for the most part ones that were familiar. Over the years a person might experience a handful of hymn festivals of the same or varied hymns, and each would be a thrilling experience. In examining hundreds of hymn festival programs over a span of four decades, one sees emerging patterns of both hymnody and improvisations. Following is an attempt to summarize these patterns and trends across the decades using representative programs.

As mentioned earlier, the hymn festivals started as organ recitals with hymnody at the beginning and end. Noting the overwhelming response to the singing of the hymns, Manz gradually reversed the order with organ music at the beginning and end, and hymns as the main portion of the festival. When the term "festival" first was used is not clear. The first mention of the term in the programs examined was in the year 1965.

What clearly comes into focus in the years leading up to hymn festivals was Manz's emerging compositional process. On the organ recital of November 20, 1960, Manz played three chorale improvisations: HYFRYDOL ("Jesus, I My Cross Have Taken"), SEELEN BRÄUTIGAM ("Jesus, Lead Thou On"), and NUN DANKET ALLE GOTT ("Now Thank We All Our God"). A brief description after each piece explained the compositional techniques used. Mention was also made that the pieces were written the previous summer and that the second one, "Jesus, Lead Thou On," would soon be published by Concordia Publishing House (Appendix 9, p. 84). [51] This corresponds to the publication date of *The Parish Organist*, Vol. 9,[52] in which this piece appeared as the only one by Manz in the anthology. The other two pieces, "Jesus, I My Cross Have Taken" and "Now Thank We All Our God," correspond to Vols. I and II of Manz's *Hymn Improvisations*, Op. 5 and Op. 7. The notation at the bottom of the composition on HYFRYDOL indicates that it was written August 3, 1960. It should be noted that they were played as literature, but mention was made in the program that they were intended to be played as preludes to the hymns they intoned (similar to the preface of the Walcha chorale preludes). The following year at the organ recital of February 12, 1961, the evening hymn at the close of the service was SEELEN BRÄUTIGAM, *The Lutheran Hymnal* (*TLH*) 562, sung with the hymn text "Round Me Falls the Night." Undoubtedly the improvisation on SEELEN BRÄUTIGAM, originally paired with "Jesus, Lead Thou On," was used to introduce the hymn.

Another cornerstone hymn used by Manz to close many of his hymn festivals was also found in many of the early programs examined. The TALLIS' CANON, sung to the words "All Praise to Thee, My God, This Night" *(TLH* 558) was sung at the November 24, 1957 organ recital. No directions for how to apportion the hymn were given, leading the author to believe that it was sung by all throughout. In the Organ Dedication Recital at Emmaus Lutheran Church, St. Paul, Minnesota, April 23, 1961 (Appendix 10, pp. 85-88), the hymn was sung at the close of the service. This time, however, directions were given: The congregation was asked to sing stanzas one and two in unison. During stanzas three and four, the traditional canon setting was used. Those sitting on the lectern side were to begin each of the stanzas with the organist while those on the pulpit side were to sing the same melody beginning one measure later. Stanza five was to be sung in harmony and stanza six in unison. Through the decades, as the hymn recurred at the end of many hymn festivals, the hymn was divided so that it could be sung in canon, and directions were given telling who should enter at what point. All would sing the doxology, which was the last stanza of the hymn. The author has recollection of Manz playing this at a hymn festival, March 14, 1976, at Capitol Drive Lutheran Church in Milwaukee, Wisconsin. With eyes closed and head bowed, Manz played the last stanza with much power. It was clearly evident that he was giving his utmost to express the words of the doxology through his playing: "Praise God, from whom all blessings flow; Praise Him, all creatures here below; Praise Him above, ye heavenly host; Praise Father, Son, and Holy Ghost."

The organ recital of April 23, 1961, once again featured three chorale preludes that would later be published in Vol. I of his *Hymn Improvisations, Op.* 5, this time listing them by their hymn titles: "All Glory be to God on High" (ALLEIN GOTT IN DER HÖH SEI EHR), "Comfort, Comfort, Ye My People" (FREU DICH SEHR), and "Open Now Thy Gates of Beauty" (NEANDER).

At the organ recital of March 24, 1963, (Appendix 11, pp. 89-92), Manz performed his partita on the stanzas of ST. ANNE, "O God, Our Help in Ages Past." (The story of how he expanded this partita in a remarkable event at Valparaiso University a few weeks later is recounted below.) Though the program from the 1964 organ recital was not available, it is assumed that the improvisations would have been played before each stanza of the hymn. This partita, always wedded to the hymn, would become one of the most frequently played during the hymn festivals. The author recalls Manz's presentation to the Milwaukee Lutheran Church Musicians Guild in the fall of 1969 when these improvisations were used as models to learn how to improvise. As a fourteen-year-old boy in his first year of organ lessons, the author was spellbound!

Throughout the lifespan of *The Lutheran Hymnal,* Manz always sought out the best of its hymns for use in the hymn festivals, always cognizant of the weight of theology they contained. Often times the festivals were based on the church year. In doing so, they told "the whole story" of salvation by grace through faith in Christ Jesus. The hymnal itself is arranged according to the church year, the rhythm of worship for those in the Christian Church. Each season held special significance. Advent's promise of a Savior found fulfillment in the birth of Christ at Christmas. Epiphany heralded the good news of salvation now being preached to all nations. Lent recalled Christ's suffering and death to redeem a fallen creation. Easter, the chief festival of the Christian church year, celebrated the glorious resurrection of Christ from the dead, thereby assuring that all who believe in Him will also rise on the last day to life everlasting. Pentecost marked the birth of the Christian Church as the Holy Spirit was given to the disciples with a rushing wind and tongues of fire. The disciples were strengthened to go forth and carry out Christ's words of Great Commission: "Go therefore and make disciples of all nations, baptizing them in the name of the Father and of the Son and of the Holy Spirit, teaching them to observe all that I have commanded you; and lo, I am with you always, to the close of the age" (Matthew 28:19-20). The hymn festivals based on the church year gave the participants the opportunity to celebrate the entire church year condensed into one hour. As such, they could sing the best hymn or hymns of each portion of the church year, and have the added blessing of hearing the entire story of salvation read and sung in one hymn festival. Arranging the hymn festival according to the church year was a natural and immediately successful way to plan. The paradigm of celebrating the church year in readings and hymns was forever fresh.

The pattern of the church year gave rise to the use of "Savior of the Nations, Come" (NUN KOMM, DER HEIDEN HEILAND) for Advent, "Good Christian Men, Rejoice" (IN DULCI JUBILO) for Christmas, "O Sacred Head, Now Wounded" (O HAUPT VOLL BLUT UND WUNDEN) for Lent, "Jesus Christ, My Sure Defense" (JESU, MEINE ZUVERSICHT), "Awake, My Heart, With Gladness" (AUF, AUF, MEIN HERZ), and "Christ Jesus Lay in Death's Strong Bands" (CHRIST LAG IN TODESBANDEN) for Easter, "A Hymn of Glory Let Us Sing" (LASST UNS ERFREUEN) for Ascension, "For All the Saints" (SINE NOMINE) for All Saints, "A Mighty Fortress is Our God' (EIN FESTE BURG) for Reformation, "O

God, Our Help in Ages Past" (ST. ANNE) for End Time, to name but some of the possibilities that were found many times in the programs examined.

Hymns of praise such as "Open Now, Thy Gates of Beauty" (NEANDER), "Praise to the Lord, the Almighty" (LOBE DEN HERREN), "Praise the Almighty, My Soul Adore Him" (LOBE DEN HERREN, O MEINE), "Oh, That I Had a Thousand Voices" (O DAS ICH TAUSEND ZUNGEN HÄTTE), "Jesus, Priceless Treasure" (JESU, MEINE FREUDE), and "How Lovely Shines the Morning Star" (WIE SCHÖN LEUCHTET) also became staples of the hymn festivals, introduced with blazing improvisations. Manz interpreted internal stanzas of the hymns with energy and precision. Once again the improvisations that sprang from these hymns were later printed in his sets of *Hymn Improvisations*.

The hymn festivals of the late 1960s and early 1970s received a broadening of the hymn corpus with the publication by Concordia Publishing House of the *Worship Supplement* in 1969, (to be discussed later). Manz was at the vanguard with these hymns, giving them the best possible chance of succeeding by using them at the LCMS convention in Denver, Colorado, July 11-17, 1969 (Appendix 12, pp. 93-94). Not only were they used in the context of worship, but specific places were set aside during the liturgies, such as during the distribution of Holy Communion and the receiving of the offering, where Manz played the improvisations. Though the specific improvisations were not mentioned, one could assume that these new hymns were the basis for his improvisations.

A wealth of hymnody now found its way into the hymn festivals and subsequent volumes of hymn improvisations (Appendix 13, p. 95). These were available for the first time for many who had grown up with *The Lutheran Hymnal*. Many came to know these hymns first by hearing or playing the improvisation written for them. They carried sturdy, theologically rich language and were a delight to sing. Volumes V, VI and VIII of his *Hymn Improvisations* contain improvisations on these hymns which became staples in the hymn festivals right up to the very end in the late '90s. "God of Grace and God of Glory" was ever new and fresh in the minds of the listeners.

They came to the hymn festivals with hopes of singing the hymns as well as hearing the improvisations.

THE ATTENDANT ORGAN LITERATURE

Though hymn festivals had become immensely popular and Manz played them in copious numbers across the United States and abroad, he did not abandon his gift of playing the standard organ literature. On the contrary, he used the prelude, offertory, and postlude to play an astounding corpus of some of the best and most demanding organ literature written. His love for the music of his mentor, Flor Peeters, was shown in his use of Peeters' *Suite Modale*, Op. 43, a four-movement suite comprising the following movements: 1. Koraal, 2. Scherzo, 3. Adagio, and 4. Toccata. Manz would use a portion of the suite at the start of the hymn festival, another movement at the offering, and another movement at the end. Other representative works were also used (Appendix: 14, p. 96).

THE IMPROVISATIONS

Many came to hear of Paul Manz through his hymn improvisations, published in various volumes first by Concordia Publishing House, the official publishing house of the Lutheran Church–Missouri Synod, and later by MorningStar Music Publishers. It is safe to say that the hearing and playing of these improvisations may have drawn people to Manz's hymn festivals. They wanted to experience them from his hands as well as having the opportunity to sing the hymns which they were introducing or interpreting. Manz was asked how his improvisations evolved from playing them to writing them in finished form. He replied,

> Well, I studied the text and tried to find a key that would illustrate or trigger a musical response. I remember going through it. Even when I was on tour and I would do a hymn festival and it was advertised as a hymn festival, the congregation would submit a list of hymns from which I could gather, perhaps ten hymns at the most. From that I would then think about it before I would play that hymn festival and get some ideas. But then when I got to that organ to practice I had no ideas, but I would feel around and play that hymn until something gelled and then came

off. In most cases this was recorded and later I played it back, copied out what I wanted, and went on from there.[53]

During improvisation lessons at The Evangelical Lutheran Church of St. Luke in Chicago in the mid-1990s, the author paged through Manz's organist's edition of the *Lutheran Book of Worship*, the hymnal used at St. Luke's. There he saw thematic sketches at the tops of some of the hymns which Manz had put down as ideas for improvisations as hymn intonations or "organ only" stanzas of hymns where the organ interpreted the words of the stanza. Manz was insistent that this author should record what he played and listen to it afterward, much in the same way Manz did as he improvised.

The author recalled to Manz a time in the mid-'70s when he heard Manz play a hymn festival at Valparaiso University. One of the hymns was "My Song Is Love Unknown." Manz had a published improvisation on the stanza that begins, "They rise and needs will have my dear Lord made away." That night, however, he performed a totally different improvisation, caught up in the words of irony, "A murderer they save, the Prince of Life they slay." Needless to say, it was very moving, especially since it was a departure from what those who knew the published improvisation had anticipated. To the author's knowledge, and after checking with the university, the festival was not recorded. The improvisation was for the moment and will never be duplicated. Manz responded,

> Well, that's the way it goes. You improvise and all of a sudden you strike a note or an idea and the window opens up and you jump through the window and keep on playing with this new idea that just came to you, and you hope you're going to float in space until it's all over with.[54]

Ruth recalled, "I remember Paul saying that there is spirit (Spirit?) that seems to wash from the organ off through the chancel through the congregation, and that spirit seems to enliven whatever is going on."

Manz concurred, "Well, that's particularly true in playing the hymn itself. You get a response from the congregation to the way you're playing. That inspires me to do something else yet in the harmonization of the hymn that they're singing."[55]

He continued,

> When I got enough courage, I just went from text to music. And so if I were on tour and I was doing a hymn improvisation on "My Song Is Love Unknown," my improvisation in Milwaukee would be this, but by the time I go through Pekin, Illinois, or wherever three days later, it would be the same tune, but a different improvisation because I had lived with it for a couple of days. Something else triggered my attention or sparked myself. Don't ever stop in the middle of improvising. Because when you do this, you break the mould. Now try and recover. It's very difficult. (The author remembers those two words spoken again and again in lessons, "Don't stop!") Eventually you'll find your way out of it if you have enough vocabulary of what others have done in writing that sinks into your being, and if you get stuck you just play, play, play, and the others will emerge. It will come.[56]

Ruth added, "That is why Paul has always stressed the literature so much. Become familiar with the literature."[57] It is a skill that found its place through the broadening experience of studying piano with Richard T. Rohlfing at River Forest.

Ruth further noted that this is a kind of little quarrel that people have with Paul because they would say, "You don't play what you've written." As he plays it, he doesn't play from the printed page, he just *plays* it.

When asked to relate how he began to improvise publicly, even though he had done it more-or-less privately within the friendly confines of Mt. Olive, Manz recalled a unique moment at Valparaiso University.

THE VALPARAISO INCIDENT

> Theodore Hoelty-Nickel, Professor of Music at Valparaiso University, had a liturgical music conference, and I got a post card, literally a postcard, from him saying we are going to have this program and we're going to have it on improvisation for the church year [April

18-21, 1963] (Appendix 15, pp. 97-99). Would you be on the panel? And I said yes. What am I supposed to do? Hoelty-Nickel said, "Well, if you come to the meeting on the day of the conference, I'll take you to lunch, and the other three people who are going to improvise will be there too." The others were Philip Gehring, Professor of Music and University Organist at Valparaiso; Grigg Fountain, from Northwestern University; and Michael Schneider from Berlin, Germany. So we came for lunch, and Hoelty-Nickel said what he would like to have done, how we would talk about how we improvise and so forth.

When we got up to the balcony at Valpo, Hoelty-Nickel said, "Michael, you take, 'Schmücke dich, o liebe Seele,'" and I was scared, because he was going to announce something to me. He said to me, "You do 'O God, Our Help in Ages Past.'" So I did. Fortunately a month or two before (actually 26 days earlier, March 24, 1963, in an organ recital at Mt. Olive—Appendix 11, pp. 89-92), I had done something on "O, God, Our Help in Ages Past" at Mt. Olive for the hymn. It was just off the cuff. And this is how my partita on this hymn got going. I just improvised the entire partita on the spot.

When I was finished, M. Alfred Bichsel, Professor of Music at Eastman, who was in the back row, jumped up on the pew and just shouted, screamed, came climbing over the pews in front of all these people and hugged me and said, "I thought this art was dead, but it's very much alive." [This is reminiscent of what the aged Reinken said after Bach improvised for over one-half hour on "Schmücke dich, o liebe Seele." Manz remembered that anecdote about Bach when the parallel was mentioned.] I was just dumbfounded with the response. Now true, I had done it a week or so before (March 24), but not to that extent I had done maybe one verset at that church service (recital); at Valpo I did the entire partita.[58]

CHAPTER FOUR

A Denominational Controversy

TENSION OVER HYMNALS

The Lutheran Church–Missouri Synod is a doctrinally sound, conservative church body. "Since the time of the Reformation, three books, it has been said, have been the principal shapers of Lutheran piety. Of these three books—the Bible, the catechism, and the hymnbook—one might reasonably argue that it is the hymnbook, certainly the most regularly and frequently encountered, that has had the most enduring and lasting influence."[59] The first Lutheran pastor to come to the New World, Henry Melchior Muhlenberg, strove to take the many disparate hymnals that came over to the United States in the late 1800s, and combine them into one unified book. In his preface to the first Lutheran hymnal fashioned in America he writes, "It should be noted what until now has hindered a complete unity in connection with singing in our public worship namely the many kinds of hymnbooks, since in almost every one, various little alterations have been made, and in some of which there are few hymns, in others many. If only there were one hymnbook for all the American [Lutheran] congregations which would contain the best of the old and new spiritual songs, how much more convenient it would be."[60] In other words, doctrinal unity is necessary in a denomination's hymnal.

Throughout the decades and centuries of Lutheranism, as new hymnals were fashioned, the *kernlieder*, or core hymns of the Reformation, as found in the *Babst Gesangbuch* of 1545, were found in various amounts, from a high of 44 in the *Babst Gesangbuch* to a low of zero in Quitman's *Collection of Hymns* of 1814, which was a Lutheran hymnal.

When Manz graduated from Concordia in 1941, *The Lutheran Hymnal* came into use by the Missouri Synod. While the usual life span of a hymnal is twenty years, this one lasted until 1978 when *Lutheran Book of Worship* was published, or 1982 when its LCMS revision, *Lutheran Worship*, was published. Throughout the course of the lifespan of *The Lutheran Hymnal,* the Missouri Synod sought to update and revise it, with the eventual hope of replacing it in due time.

By the beginning of the 1960s there were two Lutheran hymnbooks serving the vast majority of Lutherans in America. The *Service Book and Hymnal* of 1958 served the Lutheran Church in America and the American Lutheran Church; *The Lutheran Hymnal* of 1941 served the Lutheran Church–Missouri Synod and those groups which had been associated with it in the Synodical Conference.

As early as 1956, however, the Missouri Synod had been considering a revision of *The Lutheran Hymnal*, then only 15 years old. However, in the years preceding 1965, the Missouri Synod had begun to take a stance of somewhat greater openness toward other Lutherans, and by the time of the 1965 convention the time seemed ripe to encourage a more cooperative approach to the matter of the revision of *The Lutheran Hymnal*.[61]

Instead of approving a unilateral revision of the hymnal, the Synod extended its hand of fellowship to the other Lutheran bodies to work toward, under a single cover: "a common liturgical section in rite, rubric, and music; a common core of hymn texts and musical settings; and a variant selection of hymns, if necessary."[62] It was further resolved that the Synod pledged its "joy, willingness, and confidence to the other Lutheran bodies as work in cooperative project begins."[63]

This was a huge step forward toward attaining Muhlenberg's goal of a common hymnal. The different church bodies approached the project with great vigor, sending their most gifted and dedicated theologians and musicians to bring such a huge undertaking into focus.

The result of this collaboration was the formation of the Inter-Lutheran Commission on Worship (ILCW), which met for the first time in Chicago, November 29-30, 1966. The work that had been started on revising *The Lutheran Hymnal* was brought to the table and fashioned into *Worship Supplement* in 1969. This would prove to be very fertile ground for Manz with new hymns to introduce within his hymn festivals and even the LCMS convention in Denver in the summer of 1969.

The ILCW published a series of booklets entitled *Contemporary Worship*. Among these were two small collections of hymns: *Contemporary Worship 1: Hymns* (1969), containing 21 hymns, five from *Worship Supplement;* and *Contemporary Worship 4: Hymns for Baptism and Holy Communion* (1972), containing 30 hymns, 4 of which were from *Worship Supplement.*

All of this was moving toward the culminating work of years of collaboration: the *Lutheran Book of Worship* (1978). Muhlenberg's dream was within arm's length. But the dream was not to be realized. Beginning already in 1969, with the election of a decidedly more conservative Synodical president and the ensuing years of theological turmoil in the Missouri Synod, voices began to be raised questioning the entire cooperative project that had been begun at the Missouri Synod's initiative in 1965.[64]

In the 1977 convention of the Synod, the Missouri Synod pulled out of the project in favor of a revised version of the hymnal. Questions had been raised about false doctrine in *LBW,* though no false doctrine was ever found. Since the Synod was bound by its own constitution to use only "doctrinally pure hymnbooks" (Art. VI, par. 4), the question remains as to why the hymnal couldn't be used in Missouri Synod congregations. A year after the revised book, *Lutheran Worship,* was issued in 1982 by the Missouri Synod, the committee that had examined *LBW* for false doctrine found none and reported its findings.[65] It was left to the imagination of those who labored so faithfully within the Synod to produce these materials as to why the book was not approved. Behind all of this stood the question of fellowship with those of other denominations with whom the Lutheran Church–Missouri Synod was no longer in fellowship.

CROSSROADS

In 1969, an even greater crisis had arisen, precipitating the hymnal controversy and leading to the fracture of the Missouri Synod and formation of a new church body. It is ironic that this happened at the LCMS convention in Denver, Colorado, for which Manz was the organist (Appendix 16, pp. 100-101). The "decidedly more conservative Synodical president," the Rev. Dr. J.A.O. Preus (1920-1994), was elected. Earlier that year, one of the two Synodical seminaries, Concordia Seminary, St. Louis, Missouri, elected a new president, the Rev. Dr. John H. Tietjen (1928-2004), a more moderate theologian. Tietjen was suspended as president over doctrinal concerns.

On February 19, 1974, forty-five out of fifty faculty members and a large majority of the students walked off the campus of Concordia Seminary and formed a new seminary, Seminex, short for "seminary in exile." They were not to return. There was no turning back. Tietjen describes the events of the day:

> I saw the procession of faculty and students was being led by a crucifix, and I listened as the procession participants sang what had become the song of the Missouri Synod's confessing movement, "The Church's One Foundation." Students and faculty moved from the quadrangle through the archway to the entrance area in the parking lot in front of the statue of Martin Luther. As they did so, they intoned Luther's hymn, "A Mighty Fortress Is Our God." Standing at the top of the entrance steps, faculty member Alfred von Rohr Sauer read a Scripture lesson from the Book of Lamentations, and Gerald Miller read the students' Seminex resolution. Then students boarded up the entrance to CS [Concordia Seminary] with two huge frames cut to fit the dimensions of the Gothic archway. Written across the two boards in large white letters on a black surface was the single word: EXILED.[66]

One cannot overstate the overwhelming emotion of that day, which had been building for quite some time. Tietjen noted the irony of the day, since it had been one year ago to the day that the previous seminary board had announced its decision "to 'commend' every member of the faculty as faithful to their commitment to the Scriptures and the Lutheran Confessions."[67] Both sides of the controversy felt they were right and just in the decisions made. There was no gray area in the matter.

Manz supported the cause of Seminex and began to play hymn festivals that benefited Evangelical Lutherans in Mission (ELIM). This organization was formed after the LCMS convention in 1973, soon after Dr. Tietjen was suspended as seminary president on charges of false doctrine. The tension within the Synod at that time was palpable. Emotions ran high. Reaction of some in the synod to Manz's activities was swift. "In September 1975 Harvey Stegemoeller, president of Concordia College [now University] in St. Paul, Minnesota, resigned rather than implement the governing board's disciplinary measures against faculty members who supported ELIM, notably world-renowned organist Paul Manz, who refused to discontinue his practice of playing benefit recitals for ELIM." [68]Seeing the dedication of Manz's organ improvisation on "God of Grace and God of Glory" to Harvey Stegemoeller gives new meaning to the words from the hymn: "Cure your children's warring madness." Stegemoeller stood firm, as did Manz, who now had added impetus for his hymn festivals: the survival of the fledgling seminary and a new church body, soon to be the Association of Evangelical Lutheran Churches (AELC). The AELC later became a part of the Evangelical Lutheran Church in America (ELCA).

One hymn which came to prominence during this crisis was "The Church's One Foundation" (AURELIA). As mentioned earlier, seminarians sang the hymn as they left campus during the walkout. In many ways it became a battle cry and a rallying point for those involved. Manz wrote a concertato on the hymn for organ, choir, brass quartet, oboe, and congregation. It was sung in ever increasing measure as this crisis unfolded. Especially fitting and poignant was the following stanza:

> Though with a scornful wonder the world sees her oppressed,
> by schisms rent asunder, by heresies distressed,
> yet saints their watch are keeping; their cry goes up,
> "How long?"
> And soon the night of weeping shall be the morn of song.
> (LBW 369:3)

Evidently this stanza struck a nerve on many levels with all concerned during this time. The editors of *Lutheran Worship* (1982), the Missouri Synod's authorized revision of *Lutheran Book of Worship*, chose to omit this stanza entirely from the hymn, although it had been in *The Lutheran Hymnal.* The Synod's most recent hymnal, *Lutheran Service Book* (2006), once again includes this stanza.

ANOTHER CALL FROM MT. OLIVE

In the midst of all the upheaval and controversy within the Synod, Mt. Olive stepped to the fore and issued another "solemn call" to Manz, who had resigned his position at Concordia in 1976. It was to be Minister of Music to the World. The people of Mt. Olive, who for thirty years had come to love Manz and be nourished by him through his playing, knew that his gift was too incredibly special to keep to themselves. Now no longer a Missouri Synod congregation, but a church affiliated with the Evangelical Lutheran Church in America, a decidedly more liberal and ecumenically minded church body, Mt. Olive saw an opportunity to undergird Manz in his *Lebenslauf,* (life's journey), to share the Gospel pan-denominationally throughout the church. When asked if Mt. Olive ever put constraints on him as to how often he could be gone, Manz simply replied, "No."

AN ECUMENICAL DOOR OPENS

The ecumenical door had been opened, and it is perhaps ironic, perhaps not, that Manz was now freed to do that for which he had been chastised and almost expelled while a high school student at River Forest—play in a church of another denomination. "Still [as] a freshman in high school, I played an organ recital in a large Roman Catholic church, whereupon the Lutheran Ministerium of Cleveland, Ohio, wrote a letter of protest to the President of Concordia College, River Forest, Illinois, and accused me of 'unionism.' I was called to the President's office one evening and was threatened with expulsion."[69] By playing in churches of other denominations, he embraced not only the hymnody of that denomination, but carried with him the best of the Lutheran *kernlieder.* This was the music that had nourished him from childhood, which he had played faithfully for decades, both in service playing and in hymn festivals. He was now able to share these hymns throughout the Christian Church, playing them each time as if they were brand new. The new paradigm was reciprocal—he culled the best from the other denominations' hymnals; the other denominations were introduced to the core hymns of the Reformation in hymn playing of the highest caliber. Manz was following the Great Commission, "And He [Jesus] said to them, "Go ye into all the world, and preach the gospel to the whole creation" (Mark 16:15).

EXPANSION OF THE HYMN CORPUS

The controversy that surrounded the publication of the *Lutheran Book of Worship* (1978) did not dissuade those who chose it as their congregation's hymnal from expanding their hymn corpus. In it they found not only the *kernlieder* and other hymns with which they were familiar, but, as is always the case with a new hymnal, also brand new hymnody written by contemporary hymn writers and musicians as well as extant hymns that were making their first appearance in a Lutheran hymnal. *Worship Supplement* (1969), as is the case with hymnal supplements, stretched the boundaries of hymnody, allowing those charged with the task of assembling a new hymnal to see what balance of old and new would be beneficial.

Once again a new corpus of hymns was available and waiting to be taught and incorporated into the body of hymns known and loved by those using the hymnal. Manz seized the opportunity to bring new hymns to the fore, now working with a hymnal that was much more pan-Lutheran than *The Lutheran Hymnal,* since it was a joint project of four Lutheran Synods (Appendix 17, p. 102). Many found their way into the hymn festivals and their attendant improvisations into the series of *Hymn Improvisations. Worship Supplement* and *Lutheran Book of Worship* had provided at least 32 new hymn tunes and texts for use within Lutheran circles and beyond. The author recalls the new life that it breathed into the rhythm of congregational worship. Manz's treatment of the hymns and attendant improvisations once again helped favorably establish the hymns in the congregation's repertoire.

THE LUTHERAN SCHOOL OF THEOLOGY/ ST. LUKE'S, CHICAGO

In 1981 the Seminex board proposed a merger of the Lutheran School of Theology in Chicago and Seminex. Eventually Seminex would be deployed three ways: (1) to LSTC, (2) to Pacific Lutheran Theological Seminary in Berkeley, California, and (3) to Wartburg Theological Seminary in Austin, Texas. Since leaving Concordia–St. Paul, Manz had continued to play hymn festivals with Mt. Olive as his base of operations and the congregation that held his call. That was soon to change. Tietjen explains,

> The proposal to invite Paul Manz to become a member of the Seminex faculty emerged out of a planning session while Seminex was still in St. Louis and we were preparing for deployment. Early in January 1983 Manz became a topic of conversation at a working luncheon for four of us who were going to share administrative responsibilities for Seminex in its deployed state. We were talking about ways of supporting the Seminex faculty and considering whether we could get enough support for endowed professorships. [David] Krause smiled through his blond beard and suggested that Manz's popularity might make it possible for us to fund a Paul Manz chair of music. [Jeanette] Burmeister looked wistfully at us and said, "Wouldn't it be great if we could put Paul Manz into the chair?"[70]

The members had come upon a brilliant idea. The idea was broached to Manz, who seemed favorably inclined. In February the Seminex board issued a call to Manz to join the portion of the faculty moving to Chicago in September. By April he had formally accepted. After 37 years at Mt. Olive, the Manzes were going to uproot to continue their ministry from Chicago. In addition to his position at Seminex, Manz continued his presence in parish music by accepting the position as Cantor at the Evangelical Lutheran Church of St. Luke in Chicago.

Manz continued his hymn festivals, playing them to raise matching funds for Seminex. His energy was indefatigable, his commitment strong to this cause within a cause: providing funds for the survival of the seminary while spreading the Gospel through his hymn festivals. The results were nothing short of astounding.

> For the next three and one-half years hymn festivals were at the center of our fund-raising efforts, and in four years

we sponsored eighty-nine such events and raised more than $717,000. Not only were the events rewarding financially but we also met with Lutherans and shared the Seminex spirit with them. In place after place people of the Missouri Synod told us that we provided them with the opportunity to be together again with their friends in the AELC. The people of the ALC [American Lutheran Church] and the LCA [Lutheran Church in America] came to the hymn festivals to celebrate unity.[71]

THE UNA SANCTA LITURGY

The daunting attempt to form a new church body called for a deep sense of trust, faith, and unity on the part of all involved. What better way to express that desire to be one in Christ than with a new Eucharistic service? Who better to write the music than Paul Manz? Tietjen recalls, "When in fall 1984 I raised the idea of a musical work with Paul Manz, who had become a member of the Seminex faculty a year earlier, he pulled out of his jacket pocket a letter he had received a few days earlier from Walter Wangerin [Jr.] (b. 1944), who had been a student at Seminex, proposing that the two of them collaborate in the creation of a new Eucharistic service for use at the time of the formation of the new Lutheran church and for ecumenical celebration of unity."[72] Portions of the Kyrie and Hymn of the Day were sung at Manz hymn festivals sponsored by Seminex in various locations since 1983 (Appendix 18, pp. 103-105). The service replaced the hymn festivals altogether in the 1986-1987 academic year "to gather the Lutherans of the three churches [church bodies] together to give thanks to God in advance of the formation of the ELCA."[73] Tietjen commented on the reaction to one such celebration of the *Una Sancta*, "One Holy" (taken from the words of the Nicene Creed, "I believe in *one holy*, catholic, and apostolic church"):

> With the words of Wangerin and the music of Manz, we raised our voices in doxology for the vision of unity present for us in our own new church:
>
>> One body and one Breathing Spirit,
>> One Lord, one faith, one Church made new,

One God and Father for the children:
By One in All are all in you!
All glory to you, now and ever.
All glory. Amen.[74]

LUTHERAN SCHOOL OF THEOLOGY HYMN FESTIVALS

The hymn festivals sponsored by the Lutheran School of Theology were designed by The Rev. Randall R. Lee, Associate Vice President for Development, Lutheran School of Theology in Chicago. Each year had a designated theme. Within the latitude provided by the theme, hymn festivals were arranged according to the season of the church year. Attendant readings suggested for each hymn were also carefully chosen by Lee.

Examination of these hymn festivals throughout the course of the academic year shows the rich variety of hymns used for each particular season as well as the flexibility necessary for Manz to prepare and play vastly varied programs from one location to the next. Nothing was left to chance in the advanced planning at each site. Directions were given to the host congregation or site concerning the program, the choir (often times a massed choir drawn from local congregations), rehearsal with Manz, other musicians, the reception, the offering, publicity, liturgists, ushers, bulletins, and travel logistics. Such well-ordered advanced planning eliminated many of the problems that could occur when sponsoring such a major festival.

The following representative programs from the 1987-1988, 1988-1989, and the 1989-1990 academic years will give examples of the richness and variety of the festivals.

1987-1988—Sing, My Tongue!

The theme of the hymn festival was taken from Philippians 2:5-11: "Have this mind among yourselves, which is yours in Christ Jesus, who, though he was in the form of God, did not count equality with God a thing to be grasped, but emptied himself, taking the form of a servant, being born in the likeness of men. And being found in human form he humbled himself and became obedient unto death, even death on a cross. Therefore God has highly exalted him and bestowed on him the name which is above every name, that at the name of Jesus every knee should bow, in heaven and on the earth and under the earth, and every tongue confess that Jesus Christ is Lord to the glory of God the Father."

Both representative services: April 15, 1988, and May 18, 1988, began with the hymn "Sing, My Tongue" (FORTUNATUS NEW) (Appendix 19, pp. 106-112). After that point the festivals diverged in the "Christ Jesus the Redeemer" section, with one program using "Jesus Christ is Risen Today" (EASTER HYMN) and the other using "Love Divine, All Loves Excelling" (HYFRYDOL). The variance in hymnody continued through the Christmas portion, "Being Found in Human Form," with one program using "All Hail to You, O Blessed Morn" (WIE SCHÖN LEUCHTET) and the other using "A Stable Lamp is Lighted" (SITTLER). "He Humbled Himself unto Death on a Cross" utilizes "O Sacred Head" (HERZLICH TUT MICH VERLANGEN) in one and "Were You There" (WERE YOU THERE) in the other. The varied readings and hymns made each festival unique while still fitting in the overall theme of the festival. In each instance, Manz played improvisations and accompaniments to the hymns that instilled them with new meaning. One could make a case for using either of the hymns for each section. In the opinion of this writer, examining both, he finds it difficult to know which one he would prefer. So great was the variety; so powerful was the combination of theme, reading, improvisation, and hymn!

1988-1989—Tomorrow Shall Be My Dancing Day

The theme of the hymn festival was taken from the Christmas hymn "Tomorrow Shall Be My Dancing Day" (DANCING DAY). The first verse is as follows:

> Tomorrow shall be My dancing day:
> I would My true love did so chance
> To see the legend of My play,
> To call My true love to My dance.
>
> *(Refrain)*
> "Sing oh! My love, oh! My love, My love, My love:
> This have I done for My true love.[75]

Various sub-themes are used depending on the season of the church year. In Advent, the threefold comings of Christ frame the service: He came, He comes, and He will come again. A rich variety of hymns for Advent, Christmas, and End Time (Judgment Day) brought the festival to life (Appendix 20, pp. 113-120).

The March 9, 1989, festival, which occurred during Lent, embraced the entire church year, a favorite framework for the festivals across the decades. Pertinent to the overall theme is the first hymn, "I Danced in the Morning" (LORD OF THE DANCE). The hymns that followed traced the church year and brought a rich variety, including Manz's own tune, SCHNEIDER, setting the Jaroslav Vajda (1919-2008) Christmas text, "Peace Came to Earth." With the remembrance that life is set against the backdrop of eternity, the festival concluded with three hymns whose texts culminate in heaven, "What Wondrous Love Is This" (WONDROUS LOVE): "And when from death I'm freed, I'll sing on;" "The King of Love My Shepherd Is" (ST. COLUMBA): "Good Shepherd, may I sing Thy Praise within Thy house forever;" and "Lord, Thee I Love with All My Heart" (HERZLICH LIEB): "And then from death awaken me." "Tomorrow Shall Be My Dancing Day" then joyously closed the festival—dancing framed the entire festival! Such was the genius of Randall Lee; such was the joyous playing of Paul Manz.

The April 16, 1989, program occurred during the Easter season. Under the sub-theme, "Who Then Can Separate Us from God's Love?" taken from Romans 8:35, "We Who Once Were Dead" (MIDDEN IN DE DOOD) was used. "Tomorrow Shall Be My Dancing Day" wass used second-to-the last, and the festival culminated with the Easter hymn "Now All the Vault of Heaven Resounds" (LASST UNS ERFREUEN).

The May 21, 1989, program occurred after Pentecost (Easter was an early March 26 that year). The second hymn under the sub-heading "God Gives the Son for Us in Death" was "All Glory Be to God on High" (ALLEIN GOTT IN DER HÖH), the second verse of which speaks of Christ atoning for our sins. The festival concluded with the great Pentecost hymn "O Day Full of Grace" (DEN SIGNEDE DAG), which, in the course of its stanzas, traces the entire first half of the church year and Christ's redemptive work, and then concludes, as did so many of the hymn festivals, in heaven:

"When we on that final journey go That Christ is for us preparing; we'll gather in song, our hearts aglow, all joy of the heavens sharing, and walk in the light of God's own place, with angels his name adoring."(LBW 161:5)

1989-1990 "So Much to Sing About"

The theme for this year's festivals came from a hymn that Jaroslav Vajda wrote for the 70th birthday of Manz (Appendix 21, p. 121-125). Vajda provided the background of the hymn:

> Paul Manz, world renowned organist, improviser, composer, and teacher, was celebrating his 70th birthday on May 10, 1989. A hymn commemorating this milestone in his career was commissioned by the Lutheran School of Theology at Chicago, where Dr. Manz was about to conclude his teaching career. As a friend and contemporary of Manz, I was asked to write a text befitting a citation he was to receive as Confessor of Faith at the Chicago seminary.

> Rather than write an explicit birthday hymn or one spelling out the many sacrifices a dedicated servant of Christ makes in the confession of his faith, I chose to focus on the inspiration and motivation a Christian follows in the use of one's special talents, in this case in the area of worship and music. Echoes of the scriptural passages appear in the text, coincidentally mentioning the biblical 'three-score years and ten' Manz was celebrating, yet with which every reader of Psalm 90 can identify in noting the limited opportunities one has for developing and using one's talents to the glory of God. The text ends with John's exclamation of recognition in the post-resurrection appearance on Christ at the Sea of Galilee.

> After trying several different metrical forms, I kept returning to one of my favorite hymn tunes, LOVE UNKNOWN by John Ireland, to which the final fits comfortably. The metrical pattern for 'My song is love unknown' is usually given with different line lengths, although the total number of syllables is equivalent and conforms to the phrasing of Ireland's haunting melody.

Marking my own 70th birthday twelve days before Manz, I wrote the kind of hymn text that would express my own feelings about the urgent but happy use of one's talents to the glory of God as centered in the Gift of gifts, Jesus Christ.

A new melody was written for this hymn by Paul Weber.[76]

The December 8, 1989, festival centered around four songs: Creation's Song, Mary's Song, The Angels' Song, and Our Song, held in Christ Church Cathedral in St. Louis, Missouri, (Appendix 21, pp. 121-125).

Subsequent programs were used by season without specific dates: Lent 1990, and Easter 1990 according to the available programs in the archives (Appendix 22, pp. 126-133).

The Easter hymn festival had the sub-themes "Sing to God," and "And Become My Salvation." Indeed, there is "so much to sing about."

FESTIVAL (LIFT) OF THE RESURRECTION

Unlike the season of Christmas, which appears to last only Christmas Eve and Christmas Day while the world outside the church celebrates Christmas through Advent *until* Christmas, Easter is a season that is celebrated for seven weeks. Each Sunday of Easter tells of another post-resurrection account in the life of Christ. Many congregations consider the Second Sunday of Easter (the Sunday after Easter) to be a "low" Sunday. Parishioners have had opportunities to worship on Passion (Palm) Sunday, Maundy Thursday, Good Friday, Vigil of Easter, and Easter Sunday, and thus attendance is typically low in many churches the Sunday after Easter. The Evangelical Church of St. Luke, where Manz served as cantor, ran counter to that trend. The Friday after Easter, a Festival of the Resurrection was held, centered on a designated theme. Representative samples from 1993 and 1995 illustrate the layout of the Festival, which culminated in a Manz hymn festival based on that year's theme.

1993 "Crown Him the Lord of Years" (Appendix 23, pp. 135-141)

The title comes from a line of the hymn "Crown Him with Many Crowns" (DIADEMATA): "Crown him the Lord of years, the potentate of time, Creator of the rolling spheres, ineffably sublime" (LBW 170:6). The day comprised numerous worship services: Morning Prayer, The Holy Eucharist, and Evening Prayer, interspersed with speakers who presented topics related to The Resurrection and Aging. Manz would play or ask one of his students to play for the services throughout the day. The evening banquet was followed by a hymn festival, also based on the theme of the day. One might say that the day provided nourishment for body, mind, and spirit.

The hymn festival was created by The Rev. Randall Lee in co-operation with Manz and Dr. Mark Bangert, choir director at St. Luke and director of the Liturgical Choir of the Lutheran School of Theology at Chicago, who chose appropriate readings and hymns to highlight the resurrection and its pertinence to the theme of the festival.

Hymns and attendant readings were ordered around the following sub-themes: Hope for the Years, Dwelling Secure, Endless Years, In Your Sight, Borne Away, Eternal Home, and O God. The hymns were drawn from *Be Happy, Saints, Lutheran Book of Worship,* and hymns from GIA Publications, Inc., Chicago. Readings and texts lifted the eyes and faith of the participants from this world to the life of the world to come. Hymn texts appropriately chosen included such lines as "God of the future, grant us faith, courage for ventures yet unknown" (ST. CATHERINE), "When tyrants tremble, sick with fear, and hear their death knells ringing; when friends rejoice both far and near, how can I keep from singing?" (QUAKER HYMN), "What joy to know when life is past, the Lord we know is first and last, the end and the beginning! He will one day, oh, glorious grace, transport us to that happy place beyond all tears and sinning!" (WIE SCHÖN LEUCHTET), "Time, like an ever-rolling stream soon bears us all away," and "Still be our guard while troubles last And our eternal home!" (ST. ANNE), and the theme hymn, "Crown Him with Many Crowns, (DIADEMATA), from which was taken "Crown him the Lord of years, the potentate of time, Creator of the rolling spheres, ineffably sublime. All hail, Redeemer, hail! For thou hast died for me; Thy praise and glory shall not fail throughout eternity." Those who attended were indeed lifted by what they experienced. Manz referred to this day as the *"Lift* of the Resurrection."

1995 "Celebrating the Life and Work of Dietrich Bonhöffer"
(Appendix 24, pp. 142-149)

The year 1995 marked the 50th anniversary of the death of Dietrich Bonhöffer (1906-1945), who was a German Lutheran pastor, theologian and participant in the German resistance movement against Nazism as well as a founding member of the Confessing Church. He was involved in plots planned by members of the *Abwehr* (the German Military Intelligence Office) to assassinate Adolf Hitler. Arrested in March 1943, he was imprisoned, and eventually hanged just before the end of the Second World War in Europe. His writings, among which *Letters and Papers from Prison* and *Life Together,* have ennobled Christians and enabled them to persevere amid the obstacles of life and testing of faith. As such, these and other writings of his became marvelous material to be used in the "Lift" of the Resurrection.

The author was privileged to be asked to play for Evening Prayer. Hymns were chosen from the recently published supplement to *Lutheran Book of Worship, With One Voice,* giving participants one of their first chances to sing the new hymns.

The hymn festival was based on the title of Bonhöffer's book, *Life Together.* The combination of such eloquent, powerful writing and a rich assortment of new hymns, all taken from *With One Voice,* shaped and crafted by Manz, made for an evening of powerful singing and many moments of emotional response. The thought of Bonhöffer hanging by piano wire as the price paid for his beliefs and actions brought one type of feeling. The clarity of the Gospel message in the face of all evil and Christ's assurance to his disciples, "In the world you have tribulation, but be of good cheer, I have overcome the world," (John 16:33b) brought a different kind of emotion—one of wonder and awe.

FURTHER EXPANSION OF THE HYMN CORPUS

Approaching the twilight of his ministry, Manz was once again gifted with a fresh infusion of hymns into the hymn corpus of the Lutheran Church. In 1995 the Evangelical Lutheran Church in America published *With One Voice,* a supplement to the *Lutheran Book of Worship,* which had been published in 1978. The title *With*

One Voice held significance for the ELCA on more than one level in that it is based on Romans 15:5-6: "May the God of steadfastness and encouragement grant you to live in such harmony with one another, in accord with Christ Jesus, that together you may *with one voice* [emphasis the author's] glorify the God and Father of our Lord Jesus Christ." The title was also used during the seminary controversy.

> The students who were involved with Seminarians Concerned were hard at work during the Day of Theological Reflection, calling on their fellow students to take responsible action. On the basis of the discussion that day, fourth-year student David Abrahamson worked overnight to compose a document to serve as a theological foundation for united students' action. Entitled "With One Voice," the document was submitted for signature to CS students, given to the BoC [Board of Control: the governing board of Concordia Seminary] and distributed to all pastors and teachers of the Missouri Synod. Ultimately, 450 students signed the document.[77]

With One Voice had a stronger ethnic emphasis and, as was the case with *Worship Supplement* in 1969, it pushed the boundaries of hymnody, "testing the waters" to see what could be included in the hymnal that would succeed the *Lutheran Book of Worship.* Manz embraced some of which he had already used from other publications (Appendix 25, p. 150). The intonation to "I Want to Walk as a Child of the Light" (HOUSTON) particularly stands out as one in which Manz reaches back to his past and weaves it into the hymn tune. The text stresses a childlike faith and a desire to walk as a child of the light, following Jesus. Within the intonation Manz intertwines the German Christmas tune *"Ihr Kinderlein, kommet"* ("Oh, Come, Little Children"), a carol he undoubtedly knew and sang from childhood on in German. Here the past and the present meld, and the effect was one which brought a childlike trust and faith to the fore of those preparing to sing. The author experienced it at a hymn festival at Grace Lutheran Church during Concordia–River Forest's annual "Lectures in Church Music," publicly reading the following text (1 John:3:8-10) immediately preceding the hymn: "Yet I am writing you a new commandment, which is true in him and in you, because the darkness is passing away and the true light is already shining. He who says he is in the light and hates his brother is in the darkness still. He who loves his brother abides in the light, and in it there is no cause for stumbling." Manz was ever searching for ways to bring fresh awareness to a hymn text. In this instance he succeeded beautifully.[78]

RECONCILIATION

Manz garnered many awards and recognitions over the years including the Pi Kappa Lambda Award by Northwestern University in 1952, the Saint Cecelia Award by Boys Town in 1966, the Gutenberg Award by the American Bible Society in 1990, the Wittenburg Award—First Art Award by the Luther Institute in Washington D.C., in 1994, and named one of the 100 Most Notable Organists of the 20th Century by the American Guild of Organists in the year 2000.[79]

He was awarded nine honorary doctorates. Two of the more significant ones were given by LCMS universities. The first was awarded by Concordia University, St. Paul, Minnesota, in 1993, where he had labored so faithfully for so many years before leaving during the controversy. The second was Concordia University Chicago, in 1999, his alma mater, for whom he had written the *alma mater*—both words and music—in 1941, while a student. The writer feels these were olive branches—a reaching out of the institutions that helped mold him and ones that he helped to mold. It signaled an end to the strife that led to his departure from St. Paul and affirmed his ministry of servanthood to the LCMS and to the Church at large.

DENOUEMENT

Denouement is the word that Ruth Manz used to label the year 2000. The term implies that the Manzes concluded their ministry in Chicago and returned to the Twin Cities June 27, 1998. Hymn festivals after that time were privately arranged. Though no accurate count was ever kept of the number of hymn festivals Manz played year by year, Ruth was able to come up with the following numbers: 12 in 1998 and 31 in 1999 (at the age of 80!). As his former pupil, the writer stayed in contact with him and learned that all of 2000 was already booked. One of the master classes and hymn festivals was to be at Northwestern University. It was not to be.

Mary Bode, Manz's daughter, relates the following:

> The last hymn festival was to be Sunday, May 21, 2000, 3:30 P.M., at St. James Episcopal Church in Hendersonville, North Carolina. Van Kussrow (now deceased), the organist at St. James, had scheduled the hymn festival.[80] Ruth and I accompanied Paul to piggyback a visit to Ruth's aunt who was living nearby in Black Mountain, North Carolina. When Ruth called Paul Friday night to check in, he said he was not feeling well and had no energy to talk. Concerned but not overly so, we returned Saturday morning as planned to find Paul in bed, so weak he was unable to walk or talk. Dr. Harvey, our host, carried Paul to his Volvo and drove us all to the Hendersonville Hospital where Paul was admitted in Urgent Care. Tests and more tests were done. Paul's condition puzzled doctors. Father Viola of St. James Church conducted services of healing for Paul many times. Paul's fever spiked for a day to 105-106 degrees even with medication and lying on a mattress emulating a bed of ice, a fire-like rash covered his entire body, his eyes sensitive to light, sleeping all the time. Rocky Mountain Fever? Tick bite? What was this? Hospitalized for two weeks at Hendersonville, Ruth was at his side 24/7. Flying home accompanied by son John, with oxygen and a wheelchair, he slowly gained strength back home in Minnesota. The mystery of what struck him so suddenly was *never* solved.[81]

Subsequent surgeries followed, and Manz never played again. In a phone conversation with the author, Manz said that he was editing works and involved in composing. He then made a profound but simple statement, saying, "I'm lucky." Knowing his deep faith and complete trust in God, the author knew what he meant: "I'm fortunate to still be alive and serve in whatever way God wants me to serve." Though the extremely high fever severely damaged his hearing, he was not to be dissuaded. One is reminded of John Milton's (1608-1674) poem, "On His Blindness," when thinking of Manz's health. The last line is especially poignant.

When I consider how my light is spent
E're half my days, in this dark world and wide,
And that one Talent which is death to hide,
Lodg'd with me useless, though my Soul more bent
To serve therewith my Maker, and present
My true account lest he returning chide,
Doth God exact day-labour, light deny'd,
I fondly ask; But patience to prevent
That murmur, soon replies, God doth not need
Either man's work or his own gifts, who best
Bear his milde yoak, they serve him best, his State
Is Kingly, Thousands at his bidding speed
And post o're Land and Ocean without rest:
They also serve who only stand and waite.[82]

Paul O. Manz passed away at the age of 90 on October 28, 2009. His beloved wife, Ruth, preceded him in death in July the previous year.

CHAPTER FIVE

An Enduring Legacy

What, then, is the enduring legacy of the Manz hymn festivals? The answer comprises many facets.

THE REBIRTH OF HYMN PLAYING IN WORSHIP

To be sure, hymn playing within the Lutheran Church was never dead, nor was it ever totally taken for granted. For the most part pastors chose the hymns to be used in worship with little input from musicians who received the list of hymns for the following Sunday from well in advance to the night before the service. Such advanced planning—or lack thereof—dictated to what extent the organist was able adequately to prepare the hymns for the service. Those of lesser ability felt getting through all the hymns on a Sunday just as printed was a great achievement. Thankfully, many of the hymns had multiple stanzas. Each successive stanza was played with greater accuracy. If one was industrious enough, registrations could even be changed for successive stanzas.

The hymn festivals brought a fresh—if not startlingly new—awareness of what actually could be done with a hymn with adequate preparation. The hymns were played at a steady tempo with a *tactus* that was unwavering from introduction to the last phrase of the last stanza when a broadening would occur. Registrations varied from stanza to stanza and "fit" the text of that stanza accordingly. The text of the stanza was brought to the fore, and one began to look at each stanza as a part of the whole. Organists began to read the hymn texts before playing them. "Praise the Almighty, My Soul Adore Hymn," (LOBE DEN HERREN, O MEINE SEELE) found in hymnals in the section "Praise and Adoration" is no longer played with power and bombast throughout. Organists rethink their registrations after reading the following stanza:

> Penitent sinners, for mercy crying,
> Pardon and peace from Him obtain;
> Ever the wants of the poor supplying,
> Their faithful God He will remain.
> He helps his children in distress,
> The widows and the fatherless. Alleluia! (LSB 797:4)

The plaintive, contemplative nature of the text calls for a more subdued registration. The more one reads the *entire* text of a hymn before planning to practice it, the more one finds places to alter the registrations and harmonies to elucidate the text. Attention is not drawn to the organist; attention *is* drawn to the hymn text.

Organists have been shown how to explore the tonal possibilities of their organs. Even organs with modest stop lists hold possibilities beyond what has been used in the past. Through sensitive, creative registration, new colors find their way into hymn accompaniment. The *cantus firmus* of the hymn *can* be placed in the pedal, or played on a separate manual, even with a two-manual organ. Organists have been shown how to map out registration changes for each hymn. Such advanced planning also affects the way in which the liturgy is to be played. Hymns and liturgy are no longer obstacles in the service, but events. The primary attention to prelude, offertory, and postlude has gradually shifted toward the hymns. The congregation has been the great beneficiary of these efforts. Those singing the hymns draw added meaning from the hymn texts because of the sensitive treatment given to those texts.

Manz's harmonic language of the hymn stanzas went far beyond the standard harmonies delineated in the hymnal. Ninths and sevenths were added to the chords, adding a tension in the harmony that propelled the hymn forward until some of the dissonances were resolved. The added notes—sometimes as many as seven or eight—strengthened the texture of the hymn and thereby further undergirded the singing. Not all dissonances resolved. Final chords of hymns contained ninths, sevenths, and sixths, further enriching the harmonic palette of the accompaniment. One such example is his hymn accompaniment for "Jesus Christ, My Sure Defense" (Appendix 26, pp. 151-152). Organists have begun to test the boundaries of their congregations' acceptance of such new sonorities. Feedback, whether positive or negative, is weighed in the organist's mind, and hopefully influences future performances.

Clergy also were the beneficiaries of this fresh awareness of hymns. They are now taking a closer look at hymn texts, finding those that bear a clear Gospel message and fit within the context of the worship service and the church year. Choosing a small corpus of "personal favorites" has been gradually replaced by choosing an ever broader range of hymns that contain substance rather than just emotion. Perhaps this has also led to increasing dialogue between pastor and organists as hymns are discussed and critiqued from various perspectives: substance, pertinence, and the congregation's ability to grasp and be edified by the hymns. This has not been an overnight occurrence, and, as one can imagine, has happened with various degrees of success from congregation to congregation. But it is safe to say that those who heard and reacted favorably to a Manz hymn festival never saw hymns in the same way again. A new standard of excellence, sensitivity, and awareness had been offered and was to be emulated.

It is quite possible that the role of the cantor has also seen a rebirth and elevation in importance as a result of Manz's ministry. The cantor is seen as more than one who can play or direct, but also as one who can *discern* music that is worthy of use in the Divine Service, music that can edify man as well as glorify God. It is a serious calling, remembering that music of the church is also that which carries the Gospel. Manz modeled this by keeping his calling as cantor throughout his entire ministry, refusing to be only a pedagogue, but carrying inside him a deep desire to minister to God's people through church music in the context of worship. This continued to speak volumes to aspiring organists eager to display their virtuosity in recital. Manz's virtuosity was dutifully and willingly sublimated to being a leader at worship.

At a funeral for which Manz played and the author attended as a member of the board of directors of the Association of Lutheran

Church Musicians, Dr. Philip Gehring from Valparaiso University, also a member of the board, saw Manz and greeted him simply as "Cantor Paul." This was a purposefully respectful greeting: a greeting of the man preceded by the acknowledgement of his role. It was one of two funerals the author heard Manz play. In the days of interviewing him, Manz characterized his funeral playing as a "long, triumphant cry of Easter."[83] Both funerals were exactly so.

THE SPAWNING OF IMPROVISATION AND COMPOSITION BY ORGANISTS

After the "Valparaiso incident" mentioned earlier, one of those present said that "next week one hundred musicians will try this and be fired."[84] What was meant was that musicians would try to replicate what Manz had done with "Our God, Our Help in Ages Past" with other hymns in their congregations, and fail because they didn't have adequate knowledge and skills necessary to be successful. Thankfully this statement was only partially correct. Organists—not only those attending the symposium at Valparaiso, but also those exposed to Manz's music at hymn festivals or in his published organ improvisations—*did* return to their own organ benches and dare to try. They played his music again and again, studied it, and tried to apply it to their own playing. Enthusiasm had been sparked, and they were determined to make this a part of their craft as organists. It caused them to look for resources, whether in improvisation as these came into being, or in books of altered accompaniments for hymns. It was not always necessary to create new music. Others could do that. It was their responsibility and delight to play this music to the best of their abilities. No longer were hymns played with the same harmonization throughout.

Those who were able did improvise, create alternate harmonizations for the hymns, and *publish* them. Publishers were eager to bring these pieces into print, having received numerous requests from the field as musicians scrambled to find resources to enliven their playing—both hymns and attendant literature. A steady burgeoning of hymn-related organ music has occurred in ever increasing measure since the 1970s. From the very basic to the technically demanding, these pieces mark a time in the life of the Church's hymnody that is full of vigor and energy. Preludes, intonations, improvisations, and alternate harmonies on hymns are in copious supply for every range of ability. The impetus for this renaissance lies in the genius of the Manz hymn festival.

THE PROLIFERATION OF HYMN FESTIVALS

Organists are finding legitimacy in using their talents to play hymn festivals. They see, as did Manz, that people love to sing hymns. Attendant organ music can greatly enhance these festivals, as was the case with Manz, but those attending are equally satisfied with hymn singing and participation as they are with listening to the playing of great organ literature, whether the classics, or the new pieces written by or played by the performer. Dr. Donald Busarow, Dr. Walter Pelz, Dr. David Cherwien, Dr. John Behnke, and Dr. John Ferguson are but a few of those who have sublimated playing organ recitals to playing hymn festivals. In doing so, they have given rise to composing and improvising organ music of the highest caliber. Each has also brought his unique harmonic vocabulary to bear upon the hymns used in the festivals. Students under their tutelage as well as organ students in general in religious institutions are being taught improvisation and playing alternate hymn accompaniments within their regimen of lessons. The results are exponential. Organ and composition students are producing an ever new corpus of hymn-based music.

THE PROMULGATION OF *KERNLIEDER*
TO OTHER DENOMINATIONS

Manz's ecumenical openness had a decidedly positive impact on other denominations. The *kernlieder*, or core hymns of the Reformation, were deeply ingrained into his very being. He had learned them as a boy, had them nourish and strengthen his faith in his formative years, and used them tirelessly in service playing and hymn festivals. They formed the early core of his repertoire. Moving freely among other denominations, he embraced their hymnody *and* continued to play these core hymns, much to the delight and sometimes first hearing by those in attendance. One such festival took place October 29, 1980, in Ft. Worth, Texas. University Christian

Church sponsored the festival to celebrate the fiftieth anniversary of the Ft. Worth chapter of the American Guild of Organists. A particularly handsome program handed out was a portent of the high quality of the festival (Appendix 27, pp. 153-159). Among several hymns chosen were three *kernlieder*: "Praise to the Lord, the Almighty" (LOBE DEN HERREN), "Jesus, Priceless Treasure" (JESU, MEINE FREUDE), and "O Sacred Head, Now Wounded" (PASSION CHORALE). They were on equal footing with the other "giants" in the festival. This is but one example of Manz's continued love for and use of these core hymns of the Lutheran Church.

FOUNDATION BUILDING FOR A NEW CHURCH BODY AND SEMINARY

One indelible legacy Manz leaves is the foundation of the Evangelical Lutheran Church in America and Seminex. Both were the recipient of his indefatigable energy and determination for them to succeed under God's blessings. Manz risked *everything* for that in which he believed. He was the "darling" of the Missouri Synod, at the zenith of his popularity as a leader of hymn festivals, and widely regarded as the *best* organist in the Missouri Synod. His legacy was already secure, and Manz could have stayed in his present positions at Mt. Olive and Concordia–St. Paul for ten more years and then retired. He could have stepped aside from either or both of those calls and exclusively played hymn festivals while remaining a member of the LCMS. Already having persevered through the criticism, though muffled, of his studying with a Roman Catholic (Flor Peeters), he emerged with skills of the highest caliber. Despite being equally synonymous with the Missouri Synod as he was with hymn playing itself, he was moved after much deliberation and fervent prayer to leave the Synod and side with those who also left the Synod to form Seminex, ELIM, and eventually the ELCA.

One is reminded of Abraham (in Genesis 12) being told by God to go forth, not knowing where he was going, only knowing that God was leading him. Jesus gave his disciples the same challenge (in Matthew 10), telling them not to take anything extra when they went, causing them to fully trust in God. One of the prayers in the order of Morning Prayer speaks eloquently to this same circumstance:

Lord God, you have called your servants to ventures of which we cannot see the ending, by paths as yet untrodden, through perils unknown. Give us faith to go out with good courage, not knowing where we go but only that your land is leading us and your love supporting us; through Jesus Christ our Lord.[85]

In the eyes of the Synod, it must have looked like a freefall, but it is the author's feeling that in God's eyes, it was a placing of Manz exactly where he was to bring his gifts to bear in a most marvelous way. His hymn playing emboldened those who were members of the fledgling seminary and Synod as well as those who supported them. It gave a strong sense of legitimacy to their cause to have one as devout and revered as Manz giving his all to support them. Apart from any endorsement of this religious cause, it gave him a myriad of opportunities to spread the Gospel through his hymn festivals. People who ordinarily might not have attended were drawn to the hymn festivals to support those championing the new seminary and church body. The Gospel was preached with great conviction from the organ. Manz's work was not in vain. The prophet Isaiah summarizes this activity well:

For as the rain and the snow come down from heaven, and return not thither but water the earth, making it bring forth and sprout, giving seed to the sower [sic] and bread to the eater, so shall my word be that goes forth from my mouth; it shall not return to me empty, but it shall accomplish that which I purpose, and prosper in the thing for which I sent it (Isaiah 55:10-11).

Quantifying the effect Manz had in this regard would be as impossible as quantifying the number of his hymn festivals, the number of people who heard him play, or the number of people who played his music. This side of eternity, no one could—or should—put this ministry into hard numbers.

THE EDUCATIONAL IMPACT OF HIS STUDENTS WHO NOW TEACH

Manz himself sewed these seeds through his Paul Manz Institute. Students would come to Chicago from across the United States to specifically study hymn playing and improvisation with Manz with scholarship money made available through the institute. The author was the great beneficiary of this arrangement, being one of the last students to study with him at the Evangelical Lutheran Church of St. Luke in Chicago in the mid-1990s. Imagine actually getting to study with Manz himself as he methodically took you through his curriculum that he had honed and perfected over decades of teaching and playing! His patience was astounding, his technique impeccable, his praise lavish when deserved, and his expectations high. The author was told at his first lesson, "*After* the lesson, you and I will be friends!" Often times, as the maxim goes, "What was caught was as great as what was taught." Conversations which included anecdotes and reminiscences during the lessons brought valuable insights that no textbook could contain. One of the highlights of the lessons would be when Manz would ask the rhetorical question, "May I sit down and play?" The bench was gladly vacated as he would sit down and demonstrate. Remembering what had just been improvised by his student (since no written music was ever present at the lessons) he would re-craft the piece or add a particular nuance that would make the piece come to life. Such was his genius. "There, now you try," he would say, always complimenting *during* the playing where warranted. "Good, good, excellent. Don't stop!" (The author became used to those comments booming from behind him while playing.)

Fully two generations of his students are now teaching, whether privately or in institutions of higher learning. They are perpetuating the excellence of his ideals both in organ literature, improvisation, and service playing. Those whose calling is to be that of a cantor are also teaching through their playing and directing. The attention they give to the hymns and the musical nurture of the congregation bears witness to the example by which Manz led his life of ministry in church music.

THE QUEST FOR EXCELLENCE IN MINISTRY

In his pamphlet, *The Theological Character of Music in Worship*, Robin Leaver states that "The music of worship has its roots in the past, its blossom in the present, and its fruits in the future."[86] This statement embraces Manz's idea of ministry in the hymn festivals as well as every aspect of his musical and personal life. Keenly aware that he was the keeper of a rich tradition and a vital part of that continuity, Manz, like Luther, cherished what was handed down to him. In his book *Luther on Music: Paradigms of Praise,* Carl Schalk writes about Church Music and Continuity. "Luther's understanding of continuity in worship and song suggests an attitude toward the received tradition that may be helpful today. It shows grateful thanks and appreciation for God's good gifts of hymnody, liturgy, and church music received from our fathers and mothers in the church. Many elements of that tradition have nourished the faithful for generation after generation. We receive that heritage thankfully as God's good gift to us."[87] Manz considered all of his life to be that of ministry. As such he wanted to be a vital link in this continuity. "Maybe we will find our voices and take our own place in the rich tradition of the church's music. The long procession of those who have worshipped our God over the past four thousand years forms a continuum which we join."[88]

His work in the present incorporated the best of the Church's heritage with emerging hymnody that he felt worthy of inclusion in this continuum. "We sift through the resources and offer our finest. . . . [We] are as restless as we are ruthless in search of excellence. We reserve excellence for our God. . . . It [music] is a gift of God in which we delight. And it is a treasure we offer as we lift up our hearts in worship."[89] Looking ahead to the future and an endless song in heaven with saints and angels, Manz states, "When in worship, I find energy to encourage others in their worship. Yes, there are times when the song sticks in my throat and my own heart feels like breaking. Like all ministers, like all humankind, we grieve. But even the servants in worship stand in the presence of God's grace. Because of this I translate my tears into songs. It becomes a holy privilege to facilitate the grief of others, just as it is possible to share in another's reason for rejoicing. Together we face the uncertainly of the days ahead in the holy and certain hope of God's love."[90] This privilege to minister leads Manz to sum up his life's work as follows: "By vocation I am a parish organist. I preach, but from the other end of the nave, from the organ loft." "The Biblical word is most important. . . . Music can woo people to church, but the Word will win them."[91]

Epilogue

When the author was ready to take leave of Paul and Ruth Manz after several days of interviews, and before any of the writing had begun on this document, he shared with them his thoughts about how the paper should end. As with the beginning of the paper, the end holds equally significant theological thoughts. The traditional collect for the service of Morning Prayer embodies the life and ministry of Paul Manz.

> Almighty God, grant to your Church your Holy Spirit and wisdom which comes down from heaven that your Word may not be bound but have free course and be preached to the joy and edifying of Christ's holy people, that in steadfast faith we may serve you and in the confession of your name may abide to the end; through Jesus Christ, our Lord.[92]

This, then, becomes the crowning legacy of the hymn festivals and the ministry of Paul Manz: the free course of the Gospel played and sung, preached to the joy and edifying of all who heard it, with the heartfelt desire of strengthening the faith of all who participated. May God grant the fulfillment of this prayer.

Appendices

APPENDIX 1: Edwin Arthur Kraft

APPENDIX 2: Welte-Tripp contract for organ repair. See specifications on next two pages.

No. 1012-J0

Welte-Tripp Organ Corporation hereby agrees to build and install in the

Mt. OLIVE EVANGELICAL LUTHERAN CHURCH

3049 Chicago Ave.   - - - -   Minneapolis, Minn.

One Welte-Tripp Pipe Organ

Ready for use and in accordance with the following specifications, viz:

MANUALS, compass CC to C⁴ .... 61 Notes
        Three
PEDALS, compass, CCC to G .... 32 Notes

Electro-pneumatic action throughout.
Philharmonic pitch, A 440, C 523.3.

Console:

Standard design, **Standard Welte** type, with bench.
Stop control, **Stop Keys or Draw Knobs**

Case:

No case or screen is embraced in this contract, except the console case and bench, of   finish.

Organ to be placed in two chambers sizes approximately as follows:

One chamber -

The other
chamber -

Church to build and supply organ chambers as per Architect's drawings, subject to approval of Organ Builder.

Motor and Blower:

Electric motor and blower of standard make to furnish ample and steady supply of wind, and direct current generator to furnish ample current for organ action.

Time of Completion:

Ready for use about   months after the countersigning of this contract by WELTE-TRIPP ORGAN CORPORATION.

(This completion time is not a term or condition of this contract, but is given in good faith and expectation of prompt completion, subject, however, to strikes, fires, freight embargoes, acts of Providence, and other causes beyond the control of Welte-Tripp Organ Corporation.)

SPECIFICATION OF AN ORGAN PROPOSED FOR

MT. OLIVE EVANGELICAL LUTHERAN CHURCH.

3049 Chicago Avenue   - - - - -   MINNEAPOLIS, MINN.

GREAT

			Pipes	Notes
Major Diapason		8'	73	
Minor Diapason		8'	73	73
Viol d'Gamba		8'	73	
Doppel Flute		8'	73	
Concert Flute	(Fm.Choir)	8'		73
Dulciana		8'		73
Octave	(Fm.Choir)	4'	12	73
Traverse Flute	(Fm.Choir)	4'		73
Tromba		8'	73	
Chimes			20	

Tremolo

SWELL

		Pipes	Notes
Swell Bourdon	16'	61	73
English Diapason	8'	73	
Stopped Flute	8'	12	73
Salicional	8'	73	
Voix Celeste	8'	61	
Rohr Flute	4'	12	73
Nasard	2-2/3'		61
Flautina	2'	12	61
Oboe	8'	73	
Tremolo			

CHOIR

		Pipes	Notes
Dulciana	16'	61	
Open Diapason	8'	73	
Dulciana	8'	12	73
Unda Maris	8'	61	
Concert Flute	8'	73	
Traverse Flute	4'	12	73
Twelfth	2-2/3"		61
Piccolo	2'	12	61
Clarinet	8'	73	
Harp	(Full Preparation)	8'		37
Tremolo			

PEDAL

			Pipes	Notes
Acoustic Bass		32'		32
Sub Bass	(Doppel Flute Extended)	16'	32	32
Bourdon		16'	12	
Lieblich Gedeckt	(Fm.Swell)	16'		32
Bass Flute	(Fm. Bourdon)	8'	12	32
Flauto Dolce	(Fm. Swell)	8'		32
Cello	(Fm. Gamba)	8'		32

COUPLERS

Great to Great	16'		Choir to Choir	16'
Great	8' off		Choir	8' off
Great to Great	4'		Choir to Choir	4'
Swell to Great	16'		Choir to Great	16'
Swell to Great	8'		Choir to Great	8'
Swell to Great	4'		Choir to Great	4'
Swell to Swell	16'		*Great to Pedal	8'
Swell	8' off		*Swell to Pedal	8'
Swell to Swell	4'		Choir to Pedal	8'
Swell to Choir	8'		Swell to Pedal	4'
*Reversible on Toe Pistons			Great to Pedal	4'

Mt. Olive Lutheran Church - Page 2.

ADJUSTABLE COMBINATIONS

6 Adjustable Pistons affecting Great and Pedal Stops & Couplers
6 Adjustable Pistons affecting Swell and Pedal Stops & Couplers
6 Adjustable Pistons affecting Choir and Pedal Stops & Couplers
6 Adjustable Pistons affecting Pedal Stops & Couplers & Toe Pistons
6 Universal Pistons affecting entire organ
On and Off Piston: Disconnecting couplers from manual pistons
On and Off Piston: Disconnecting Pedal from manual pistons.

ACCESSORIES

Balanced expression pedal affecting Great and Choir Organs
Balanced expression pedal affecting Swell Organ
Balanced Crescendo Pedal affecting entire organ
Crescendo Indicator
Sforzando pedal.
Sforzando indicator.
Action current indicator
Organ Bench (Adjustable).

Organ committee reserves the right to reject any bids.
Organ to be installed on or about Nov. 1st,1930.
Price to include freight, cartage and hoisting.
Organ chambers to be prepared by purchaser subject to approval of
                    Organ Builder.
No Grill or display included in this bid.
Wind trunking and conduit work by purchaser.
Power circuit to blower by purchaser.
Remote control wiring by purchaser
Remote control switch and mechanism by purchaser.

ANALYSIS

Major Diapason	Metal	73 Pipes	
Minor Diapason	Metal	85 Pipes	Unit
Viol d'Gamba	Metal	73 Pipes	
Doppel Flute	Wood	73 Pipes	Unit
Dulciana	Metal	73 Pipes	Unit
Tromba	Reed	73 Pipes	
Swell Flute	Wood	97 Pipes	Unit
Horn Diapason	Metal	73 Pipes	
Salicional	Metal	73 Pipes	
Voix Celeste	Metal	61 Pipes	
Oboe	Reed	73 Pipes	
Concert Flute	Wood	85 Pipes	Unit
Unda Maris	Metal	61 Pipes	
Clarinet	Reed	73 Pipes	
Bourdon	Wood	44 Pipes	Unit
Sub Bass	Wood	12 Pipes	

Chimes   Tubular Bells   20 Notes
20 Couplers
6 Universal Combination Pistons
24 Regular Combination Pistons
2 On and Off Combination Switches
20 Unit Switches
6 Ranks Unified

APPENDIX 3: Memorandum of agreement with M. P. Möller
Organ Company. See specification sheet on next two pages.

M.P.MÖLLER.INC.

MEMORANDUM OF AGREEMENT, Made this   day of   1952

by and between Harry O. Iverson,2510 Thomas Ave.S. Minneapolis 5
Minnesota,party of the first part and
Board of Trustees,Mount Olive Lutheran Church,31st.and Chicago Ave.
Minneapolis Minnesota, party of the second part.

WITNESSETH: That the party of the first hereby agrees to make
certain additions and changes in the organ in the above mentioned
church,according to specifications attached and which are to be
a part of this contract. To furnish and install new material
as specifiedand furnish necessary labor to complete the work.
To make the installation as soon as delivery can be had on the new
pipes.
       In consideration of the above the party of the second
part agrees to pay Harry O.Iverson,or his order, the sum of
Three Thousand One Hundred Fifty Dollars $3150.
       As follows;
       1st. Payment of 10% $315.
on signing this agreement
       2nd. Payment of 40% $1260.
on delivery of material to church
       3rd. Payment of 50% $1575.
upon completion of the installation according
to specifications. It is understood that the pipes which are
discarded shall revert to the party of the first part.
       IN WITNESS WHEREOF we have hereunto set our hands
and seals this day and year first above written.

       Party of the First Part   _Harry O. Iverson_

       Party of the Second Part

                         Board of Trustees
                         Mount Olive Lutheran Church

                         by _Edwin S. Albrecht_

                         Harry J. Mueller

M.P.MÖLLER,INC.

SPECIFICATIONS
for
Changes to be made in the Welte Organ in
Mount Olive Lutheran Church- 31st.and Chicago Ave,Minneapolis.

All stops are the present ones unless otherwise stated.

GREAT ORGAN

Diapason		8'	
Gedeckt	ch.	8'	
Dulciana	ch.	8'	
Octave		4'	present Sw.Diap. on Gamba
Spitz Principal	ch.	4'	
Dulciana	ch.	4'	
Super Octave		2'	from ch.Spitz Principal
Mixture III	-		122 new pipes on Tromba
			draws Super Octave as one rank
Tromba		8'	on Dopple Flute

SWELL ORGAN

Bourdon	16'	
Diapason	8'	present Ch.Diapason
Flute	8'	present Ch.Con.Fl. 13-24 new Chimney Fl.
Salicional	8'	
Vox Celeste	8'	
Flute	4'	new Conique 23 trebles
Nazard	2⅔'	
Flautino	2'	
Trumpet	8'	bright English- new pipes,on Oboe
Vox Humana	8'	
Clarion	4'	bright English- new pipes and action
		(or Hautbois if Schopp can obtain shallots)
Tremulant	(controls mounted on key cheek)	

CHOIR ORGAN

Gedeckt	8'	present Sw. pipes
Dulciana	8'	
Undamaris	8'	
Spitz Principal	4'	new pipes on Diap.
Flute	4'	fr.Ged. 40 new Spitz Trebles
Dulciana	4'	fr. Dul.Unit
Dulciana Twelveth	2⅔'	"
Dulciana Fifteenth	2'	"
Oboe	8'	pr.Sw. on Clarinet
Clarinet T.C.	8'	new action (Harpe Knob)
Tremulant		

M. P. MÖLLER, INC.

PEDAL ORGAN

Resultant		32'	re-wired
Sub Bass		16'	
Leib.Gedeckt	sw	16'	
Bass Flute		8'	
Flute	sw	8'	
Choral Bass		4'	
Tromba		16'	ex.Gt.Tromba-1-12 new pipes

Other provisions

Duplicate Pts. with manual piston
New Engraved Heads for stop changes
Regulate Shades and Tremulants
Reset Crescendo and Pts. pedals
Regulate and Tune all pipe work.

APPENDIX 4: Specifications for the new Schlicker organ

Schlicker Organ 1965
Mt. Olive Lutheran Church   Minneapolis, Minnesota

THE MAIN ORGAN SPECIFICATIONS:

Great Organ

16' Pommer	4' Hohlfloete	8' Trompeta Real
8' Principal	2' Octave	4' Trompeta Real
8' Spitzfloete	IV-VI Mixture	Chimes
4' Octave	16' Trompeta Real	

Swell Organ

8' Rohrfloete	4' Principal	IV-V Mixture
8' Voix Salicional	4' Koppelfloete	16' Fagott
8' Voix Celeste	2 2/3' Nasat	8' Schalmey
8' Dolce	2' Nachthorn	4' Clarion
8' Dolce Celeste	1 3/5' Terz (Tenor C)	Tremolo

Positiv Organ

8' Gedeckt	III-IV Scharf	8' Trompeta Real
4' Rohrfloete	8' Krummhorn	(Great)
2' Principal	Tremolo	4' Trompeta Real
1 1/3' Klein Nasat	16' Trompeta Real	(Great)
1' Siffloete	(Great)	

Pedal Organ

32' Resultant	4' Choralbass	16' Fagott (Swell)
16' Principal	4' Pommer (Great)	8' Trompeta Real
16' Subbass	2' Blockfloete	(Great)
16' Pommer (Great)	IV Mixture	8' Trumpet
8' Octave	32' Contra-Fagott	4' Clarion (Swell)
8' Pommer (Great)	16' Posaune	

THE ANTIPHONAL ORGAN SPECIFICATIONS

Great Organ

8' Rohrgedeckt	4' Principal	III Mixture (metal) 2'
Gemshorn		

Pedal Organ

16' Gedecktbass	8' Gedeckt (Great)	Couplers
8' Great to Pedal	4' Swell to Positiv	8' Antiphonal
8' Positiv to Pedal	16' Swell to Great	to Great
8' Swell to Pedal	8' Swell to Great	8' Antiphonal
16' Positiv to Great	4' Swell to Great	to Pedal
8' Positiv to Great	16' Swell to Swell	Antiphonal ON
16' Swell to Positiv	4' Swell to Swell	great OFF
8' Swell to Positiv		

COMBINATION PISTONS

Great 1 2 3 4 5   Swell 1 2 3 4 5   Positiv 1 2 3 4   General 1 2 3 4 5 6 7 8
General Cancel/Pistons and toe studs
Zimbelstern ON and OFF/Seven cast bells, toe stud Sforzando and Indicator light
Great to Pedal Reversible/Toe Stud   Balanced Swell expression pedal
Crescendo Pedal and indicator light   Crescendo pedal ON and OFF/Toe stud

APPENDIX 5: "Jesus, Lead Thou On"

APPENDIX 6: Franck console

APPENDIX 7: Walcha organ

Erbaut 1961 von der Berliner Orgelbau-Werkstatt Karl Schuke

Disposition der Orgel in der Dreikönigskirche, Frankfurt am Main

HAUPTWERK	OBERWERK
Quintadena 16 '	Metallgedackt 8 '
Principal 8 '	Quintadena 8 '
Spielflöte 8 '	Principal 4 '
Rohrflöte 8 '	Rohrflöte 4 '
Oktave 4 '	Quintflöte 2²/₃ '
Nachthorn 4 '	Oktave 2 '
Nassat 2²/₃ '	Nachthorn 2 '
Oktave 2 '	Terz 1³/₅ '
Flachflöte 2 '	Sifflöte 1 '
Mixtur 5–6 f.	Scharff 4 f.
Trompete 8 '	Rankett 16 '
	Krummhorn 8 '
PEDAL	– Tremulant –
Principal 16 '	
Subbaß 16 '	BRUSTWERK
Quintbaß 10²/₃ '	Holzgedackt 8 '
Oktave 8 '	Blockflöte 4 '
Gedackt 8 '	Quintadena 4 '
Oktave 4 '	Waldflöte 2 '
Koppelflöte 4 '	Sesquialtera 2 f.
Bauernflöte 2 '	Quinte 1¹/₃ '
Rauschpfeife 3 f.	Oktave 1 '
Mixtur 5 f.	Cymbel 3 f.
Posaune 16 '	Regal 8 '
Trompete 8 '	Regal 4 '
Schalmei 4 '	– Tremulant –
Cornett 2 '	
– Tremulant –	KOPPELN
	BW/HW – OW/HW
	BW/Ped. – OW/Ped.

Die Orgel hat Schleifladen mit mechanischer Spieltraktur und elektrischer Registratur, sechs General-Setzerkombinationen und eine Einzel-Setzerkombination. Das Brustwerk ist mit Jalousieschweller versehen.

30187

APPENDIX 8: A Bag of Noodles

31.

ᴼNE DAY, I HEARD A MAN SAY:
"HOW CAN YOU _NOT_ BELIEVE IN JESUS??
THE BIBLE IS FILLED WITH *PROOF!*
HE PERFORMED ALL THOSE MIRACLES,
CURED THE SICK & THE LAME, BROUGHT
THE DEAD BACK TO LIFE TO PROVE HE
WAS WHO HE SAID HE WAS !!"

OH, NO SIR, HE DIDN'T - HE NEVER
DID! THE BIBLE DOESN'T "*PROVE*" ANY-
THING & NEITHER DID JESUS. THE THRILL
IS THAT JESUS NEVER CURED TO PROVE...
HE ONLY CURED WHEN FAITH IN HIM WAS
ALREADY THERE, _FIRST._ OR JUST BECAUSE HE
WANTED TO. IT'S IN THE BOOK AND IT'S
BEAUTIFUL, BUT THE FAITH WASN'T JUST THAT
HE COULD DO MIRACLES. THE FAITH WAS IN
HIM. IN WHAT HE SAID & IN WHERE HE
WAS AT. IN WHAT HE FOSTERED. IF YOU
DIDN'T BUY THAT, AND JUST WANTED A FREE
MIRACLE FOR PROOF...FORGET IT.

I THINK THE MIRACLE IS WHEN HE
DOESN'T CURE BUT YOU STILL _KEEP_ YOUR
FAITH...EVEN THOUGH HE DECIDED THAT
YOU _KEEP_ YOUR LIMP, YOUR ASTHMA, OR YOUR
SICK CHILD. BECAUSE HE LOVES YOU.

PROOF? what's great about love is you never have to prove it!

III.

THREE CHORALE IMPROVISATIONS   Manz

HYFRYDOL (Lutheran Hymnal, 423)

SEELENBRÄUTIGAM (Lutheran Hymnal, 410)

NUN DANKET ALLE GOTT (Lutheran Hymnal, 36)

Written during the past summer, these settings are taken from a second set of IMPROVISATIONS FOR THE ORGAN and are intended to be played as preludes to the hymns they announce.

HYFRYDOL makes use of a counterpoint of light colored flutes in joyful, quiet exuberance. Interspersed is found the cantus in simple harmony.

The second improvisation will soon appear in a publication by Concordia Publishing House.

The musical language of NUN DANKET ALLE GOTT is contemporary and dissonant. Polychordal treatment and rhythmic emphasis are quite apparent.

An Organ
Dedication Recital

by

PAUL MANZ

APRIL TWENTY-THIRD

1961

Three o'Clock

Emmaus Lutheran Church

ST. PAUL, MINNESOTA

THE REV. VERNON KOEPER, *Pastor*

✠ IN NOMINE JESU ✠

ymn of Praise (Lutheran Hymnal, 250) . . . . Vienna, 1775

✠   The order of Vespers   ✠
(p. 41)

Psalm 98 (p. 144)
(Read responsively)

✠

Gloria Patri

✠

I.

E AND FUGUE IN D (DORIAN MODE) . . . . *Van den Kerkhoven (1627–1673)*
Abraham van den Kerkhoven was born in 1627 in Brabant and died in 1673 in
ssels. He was organist at the royal court of the southern Netherlands. His PREL-
E AND FUGUE IN D (Dorian mode) is a good example of the Baroque style
ı its broad sweeping lines. It foreshadows Bach and Buxtehude.

HORALE PRELUDES . . . . *Johann Sebastian Bach (1685–1750)*
Ach Bleib Bei Uns
Meine Seele Erhebet den Herren

Among the four collections of organ chorals by Bach, the Little Organ Book, the
chism, the Schuebler Chorales and the Eighteen (larger chorale preludes) — the
ıebler group is most unique. They were originally written not for organ but as
; or duets with obbligato instrumental parts for some of the 295 church cantatas
which only 190 have survived). They were published by Schuebler in 1747. It is
to imagine why Bach when given the opportunity to have some of his works
ished should not have rather submitted one of the other three collections of
n chorales. Instead he chose six of his favorite preludes and transcribed them
rgan.
he first prelude, "Lord Jesus Christ With Us Abide," is drawn from the beau-
cantata of the same name dealing with the walk to Emmaus. In the original
pears as a soprano solo with cello obbligato.
My Soul Doth Magnify the Lord" is a treatment of the TONUS PEREGRINUS
is also taken from the cantata of the same name. Special attention is called to
ıaunting flute solo for pedal at the very beginning and closing.

PRELUDE AND FUGUE IN B MINOR...*Bach*

Harvey Grace says of this work, "No other Prelude approaches the B minor in expressive qualities or surpasses it in beauty of texture and harmony." Albert Schweitzer lists this work as having been written during the composer's mature period at Leipzig. The prelude contains rich ornamentation, and rhapsodical flourishings. The writing for the pedals is especially interesting since its octave leaps during the pedal point heighten the effect of the chain of discords. The fugue falls into three sections, a group of entries, a freer section for manuals only and a final section with some fresh material including a new counter-subject.

II.

PIÈCE HÉROIQUE...*Cesar Franck (1882–1890)*

Born in Liège, Belgium, Franck became the "Father of modern French music." Moving to Paris at the age of eleven in order that he might have greater musical opportunities, Franck, obtained a succession of *Grande Prix* as a performer, although as a composer recognition came slowly. He was appointed organist at Sainte Clotilde in 1858, a post he held with highest distinction until his death.

THREE CHORALE PRELUDES...*Manz*

All Glory Be to God on High
Comfort, Comfort Ye, My People
Open Now, The Gates of Beauty

The first prelude based on the chorale of Decius (The Lutheran Hymnal, No. 237) is written in the form of a trio. Light colored flutes form a joyful, delicate embroidery against which the cantus firmus is heard.

The second prelude is based on a chorale from the Genevan Psalter (The Lutheran Hymnal, No. 61) and makes use of canonic imitation which anticipates the chorale itself. The latter appears with soft strings heard in a contemporary setting.

In the last prelude based on the hymn-tune NEANDER (The Lutheran Hymnal, No. 1), we find much joy and exuberance. Written in ternary form with a coda, the first and last sections are given over to the development of the hymn-tune itself while the middle section displays a short fugal exposition with a wedge like theme. Here, too, the musical language is contemporary and dissonances, polychordal treatment and rhythmic emphasis are quite apparent.

III.

TOCCATA ....*Monnikendam*

Marius Monnikendam was born in Haarlem, Holland in 1896 and is a composer of symphonic, choral and organ works. He seems to prefer short melodic phrases and is an experimentalist. The Toccata is modern and refreshingly different and dissonant.

ARIA . . . . *Peeters*

  Born in Belgium in 1903, Flor Peeters is organist of the Metropolitan Cathedral in Mechelen and professor of organ and composition at the Royal Flemish Conservatory of Music in Antwerp where he is also director.

THEME, VARIATIONS AND FINALE ON AN OLD FLEMISH SONG, Op. 20 . . . . *Peeters*

  According to Eric Blom, editor of the 9th edition of GROVE'S DICTIONARY OF MUSIC AND MUSICIANS, this opus stands out as one of the composer's most brilliant concert pieces. It is based on an old Flemish Christmas Song, "Let us all with pure hearts praise the sweet little child." The opus is inscribed to Marcel Dupre.

Theme

1st variation — Andante, chorale variation

2nd variation — Allegretto, liedform in canon

3rd variation — Vivo Scherzando

4th variation — Lento, contemplivo

5th variation — Allegro vivo, theme in pedal

6th variation — Adagio, ornamented chorale in soprano

7th variation — Allegro con spirito, Fugato

8th variation — Toccata, Finale

⌘   The offerings will be received   ⌘

THE EVENING HYMN (Lutheran Hymnal, 558) . . . . *'Tallis' Canon*

** The congregation is asked to sing stanzas one and two in unison. During stanzas three and four, the traditional canon setting will be used. Those sitting on the lectern side will begin each of these stanzas with the organist while those on the pulpit side will sing the same melody beginning one measure later. Stanza five is to be sung in harmony and stanza six once again in unison.

⌘   The Closing Vespers   ⌘
(p. 42)

⌘   SOLI DEO GLORIA   ⌘

An Organ Recital

by

PAUL MANZ

MARCH TWENTY-FOURTH

1963

Eight o'Clock

Mount Olive Lutheran Church

MINNEAPOLIS, MINNESOTA

THE REV. ALTON F. WEDEL, Pastor

THE REV. THEO. H. SCHROEDEL, Pastor Emeritus

IN NOMINE JESU

†

THE OPENING HYMN (Lutheran Hymnal, 39)   ·   *Stralsund, 1665*

† THE ORDER OF VESPERS (Page 41) †

PSALM 130 (Page 154))

(READ RESPONSIVELY)

†

THE LECTION

†

I.

VARIATIONS ON "MEIN JUNGES LEBEN HAT EIN END"
Jan Pieterszoon Sweelinck (1562-1621)

Sweelinck, Dutch "organistmaker" and founder of the historic North German school of organists, by his playing attracted many music lovers to the Oude Kerk in Amsterdam, 1580-1621.

These variations are surprisingly modern in style and breathe a cheerful calmness. The following translation of the 16th century text is by Wm. L. Sumner.

My young life hath an end—
My joy and sorrow too.
My humble soul quickly separates itself from the body.
My life cannot continue any longer.
It is frail; in truth it must go—
It is carried away with my grief.

WIE SCHÖN LEUCHTET DER MORGENSTERN (Lutheran Hymnal, 343)
Johann Pachelbel (1653-1706)

Pachelbel, noted Nuremburg organist, composed beautiful chorale preludes which became models for some of Bach's later creations. In this composition the melody is given to the pedals and the accompaniment is a solo flute.

PRELUDE AND FUGUE IN E FLAT   ·   *J. S. Bach (1685-1750)*

Albert Schweitzer in referring to the Prelude in E Flat makes the comment that it "symbolizes God-like Majesty" in a spacious movement presenting a contrast of massive effect, close writing and also of the tutti and solo idea as found in the Italian Concerto. In its original form, it stands as an overture to Bach's *Catechism.*

The Fugue which follows is the postlude to the *Catechism*, and through its casual allusions to "O God, our Help in Ages Past," is sometimes referred to as the *St. Anne* or *Trinity Fugue*. The beautiful flow of the opening polyphony, the contrasting second section and the possible Pentecostal energy and dignity of the finale are at once apparent. (A.E.F. Dickinson)

II.

FINALE IN B FLAT, OPUS 21 - - *Cesar Franck (1822-1890)*
Born in Belgium, Franck lived in Paris from 1833-1890. He is generally regarded as the greatest French composer and founder of the Modern French Music Movement.

The *Finale in B Flat* is the last of the *Six Pieces* published in 1862. Two main themes are employed. The first is a bold, incisive trumpet call which appears at the outset as an extended pedal solo. The second idea, in the rarely used key of A sharp major, is characterized by a descending four-note figure in the left hand and chords in the right hand. Following this serene episode, the work ends as brilliantly and as joyfully as anything Franck ever wrote.

IMPROVISATION ON ST. ANNE (Lutheran Hymnal, 123), OPUS 7
Paul Manz (1919-   )

1. Theme
2. Ornamented soprano, (stanza two)
3. Canon (stanza four)
4. Cantus in pedal (stanza six)
5. Pastorale (stanza seven)
6. Finale (stanza eight)

† The offerings will be received †

III.

BENEDICTUS, OPUS 59, NO. 9 - - - *Max Reger (1873-1916)*
A supreme master of every contrapuntal device in music, the German Max Reger became known as the "Modern Bach of the Organ." His treatment of the Lutheran Chorale in his huge library of organ compositions is a perpetual testimony of his unfaltering craftsmanship.

The BENEDICTUS, published in 1905, "is one of Reger's loveliest and most popular pieces. Its beautiful melody and rich harmony show Reger's ability as a tone colorist." (Carl Weinrich)

TOCCATA, FUGUE AND HYMN ON "AVE MARIS STELLA", OPUS 26
Flor Peeters (1903-   )

Flor Peeters, celebrated Belgian organist and composer is also Director and Professor of Organ at the Royal Flemish Conservatory in Antwerp. This stately latin hymn is set to a traditional modal melody. It has served as a basis for many stirring organ compositions. In this opus we hear the AVE MARIS STELLA in a three-fold capacity. In the *Toccata* it appears as a pedal solo and in the *Fugue* it is the subject conceived and developed in the Dorian Mode. A stretto leads to a majestic harmonization of the *Hymn*. The closing coda supplies the opening strains of the *Hymn* in carillon fashion. This brilliant work was written in 1948 and dedicated to Charles Tournemire, the famous French organist and composer.

THE EVENING HYMN (Lutheran Hymnal, 558)   -   *Tallis' Canon*

The congregation is asked to sing stanzas one and two in unison. During stanzas three, four and five the traditional canon setting will be used. Those sitting on the lectern side will begin each of these stanzas with the organist while those on the pulpit side will sing the same melody beginning one measure later. Stanza six will be sung once again in unison.

✝ THE CLOSING VESPERS ✝
(Page 42)

✝ SOLI DEO GLORIA ✝

APPENDIX 12: Denver Convention program

Minister: May the God of peace himself sanctify you wholly; and may your spirit and soul and body be kept sound and blameless at the coming of our Lord Jesus Christ. He who calls you is faithful, and he will do it. Go in ✠ peace.

All: Amen.

✠ ✠ ✠

ORGAN PRELUDE: "COME, HOLY GHOST, IN LOVE" — Flor Peeters

THE HOLY EUCHARIST — (Worship Supplement, p. 19)

CHORAL INTROIT FOR PENTECOST

CONGREGATION: THE THREEFOLD KYRIE (Worship Supplement, p. 19)

THE SALUTATION AND THE COLLECT FOR PENTECOST

THE EPISTLE: Acts 10:42-48

THE ALLELUIA AND SENTENCE BY THE CHOIR

THE GOSPEL: St. John 3:16-21

THE OFFERTORY (Worship Supplement, p. 25)

THE INTERCESSIONS

THE PREFACE AND THE SANCTUS (Worship Supplement, p. 26)

THE PRAYER OF THANKSGIVING AND THE "OUR FATHER" (Worship Supplement, p. 27)

THE PAX AND THE AGNUS DEI (Worship Supplement, pp. 27, 28)

THE DISTRIBUTION
Communicants will approach the nearest altar, receive the bread from the right corner of the altar, make the sign of the cross, proceed to the left corner of the altar for the wine, again make the sign of the cross, and return to their seats for the silent prayer.

DISTRIBUTION HYMNS: (Worship Supplement, 753 — "Now Let Us Pray," 754 — "Holy Spirit, Ever Dwelling," 755 — "Come Down, O Love Divine")

THE THANKSGIVING (Worship Supplement, p. 28)

THE SALUTATION AND BENEDICAMUS (Worship Supplement, p. 29)

ORGAN INTERLUDE — HYMN IMPROVISATIONS BY DR. PAUL MANZ
Processional by the acolytes and officiant from the worship center to the convention platform where the day's business will be conducted.

6

THE HOLY EUCHARIST
Theme: *"Patience"*

PRE-SESSION COMMUNION SERVICE
7:15 a. m. to 8:30 a. m.

THE ORDER OF CORPORATE CONFESSION AND ABSOLUTION
See the first page of this Orders of Worship booklet

✠

ORGAN PRELUDE: "WE ALL BELIEVE IN ONE GOD" — J. S. Bach

THE HOLY EUCHARIST — THREE (Worship Supplement, p. 63, beginning with the Hymn following the Confession)

A HYMN: "WHEN MORNING GILDS THE SKIES" (Worship Supplement, No. 789)

THE EPISTLE: James 5:7-11a

GRADUAL HYMN: "HOPE OF THE WORLD" (Worship Supplement, No. 749) (Gradual by the Choir: Ps. 121)

THE GOSPEL: St. Matthew 24:9-13

THE LITURGY OF THE EUCHARIST (Worship Supplement, p. 63)

DISTRIBUTION HYMNS:

"LORD ENTHRONED" (Worship Supplement, No. 764) and
"O LOVE, HOW DEEP" (Worship Supplement, No. 750)

ORGAN INTERLUDE — HYMN IMPROVISATIONS BY DR. PAUL MANZ Processional by the acolytes and officiant from the worship center to the convention platform where the day's business will be conducted.

PROCESSIONAL HYMN: "GOD THE FATHER, BE OUR STAY"

Congregation rises

Congregation

God the Father, be our Stay;
Oh, let us perish never!
Cleanse us from our sins, we pray,
And grant us life forever.
Keep us from the Evil One;

31

APPENDIX 13: *Worship Supplement* Hymns

"Lo, He Comes with Clouds Descending" (PICARDY)
"Come, Thou Long-Expected Jesus" (JEFFERSON)
"Angels We Have Heard on High" (GLORIA)
"O Little Town of Bethlehem" (FOREST GREEN)
"Gentle Mary Laid Her Child" (TEMPUS ADEST FLORIDUM)
"What Child is This" (GREENSLEEVES)
"Of the Father's Love Begotten" (DIVINUM MYSTERIUM)
"My Song is Love Unknown" (LOVE UNKNOWN)
"At the Lamb's High Feast We Sing"
    (SONNE DER GERECHTIGKEIT)
"With High Delight" (MIT FREUDEN ZART)
"Good Christian Men, Rejoice and Sing" (GELOBT SEI GOTT)
"This Joyful Eastertide" (VREUCHTEN)
"At the Name of Jesus" (KING'S WESTON)
"Thy Strong Word Did Cleave the Darkness" (EBENEZER)
"O Love, How Deep, How Broad, How High" (DEO GRACIAS)
"Holy Spirit, Ever Dwelling" (IN BABILONE)
"Come Down, O Love Divine" (DOWN AMPNEY)
"O God, O Lord of Heaven and Earth" (WITTENBERG NEW)
"Lord, Enthroned in Heavenly Splendor" (BRYN CALFARIA)
"In Thee is Gladness" (IN DIR IST FREUDE)
"Immortal, Invisible, God Only Wise" (ST. DENIO)
"God of Grace and God of Glory" (CWM RHONDA)

APPENDIX 14. Attendant Literature at Hymn Festivals

Bach: Prelude and Fugue in G (BWV 541)

Bach: Prelude and Fugue in e (BWV 548)

Bach: Prelude and Fugue in a (BWV 543)

Bach: Prelude and Fugue in E-Flat (BWV 552)

Bach: Prelude and Fugue in b (BWV 544)

Bach: Fantasy and Fugue in g (BWV 542)

Bach: Toccata and Fugue in d "Dorian" (BWV 538)

Bach: Toccata and Fugue in d (BWV 565)

Bach: Toccata, Adagio, and Fugue in C (BWV 564)

Bach: Passacaglia and Fugue in c (BWV 582)

Buxtehude: Toccata and Fugue in F

Duruflé: Variations on "Veni Creator Spiritus"

Langlais: Te Deum

Peeters: Lied to the Sun

Vierne: Final from Symphony No. 1

Widor: Final from Symphony No. 2

Widor: Toccata from Symphony No. 5.

APPENDIX 15: Valparaiso Church Music Seminar program

Church Music Seminar
and Society for Worship,
Music, and the Arts

APRIL 18, 19, 20, 21, 1963

VALPARAISO UNIVERSITY — VALPARAISO, INDIANA

VALPARAISO UNIVERSITY CHURCH MUSIC SEMINAR

THEO. HOELTY-NICKEL, Chairman

LUTHERAN SOCIETY FOR WORSHIP, MUSIC,
AND THE ARTS

WILLIAM WALTERS, Chairman

General Theme:

Contemporary Music and Arts
in the Service of the Church

PROGRAM OF EVENTS

THURSDAY: April 18 9:00-12:00 a.m. Student Union	*REGISTRATION.* *EXHIBITIONS.*
1:45- 2:00 p.m. Student Union	*OPENING SESSION LSWMA.* Dr. William Walters Chairman; Greetings, Dr. O. P. Kretzmann.

2:00- 3:00 p.m.
Student Union
	CONGREGATIONAL ATTITUDES TOWARDS CONTEMPORARY ART EXPRESSION IN THE CHURCH. Sociological aspects of contemporary church music and arts.
	    Moderator: Dr. William Walters.
	    Panel: Dr. Johannes Riedel
	       Dr. H. Grady Davis
	       Rev. Harvey L. Gustafson

3:15- 4:45 p.m.
Student Union
	CONTEMPORARY MUSIC IN THE CHURCH. 30 minute NBC radio program: "A New Song . . . Contemporary Church Music and the Gospel," Discussion
	    Moderator: Mr. Carl Schalk, Lutheran Hour.
	    Panel: Prof. Leland Sateren, Augsburg College.
	       Dr. Daniel Moe, University of Iowa.
	       Prof. Richard Hillert, Concordia College.
	HYMN SING. Composers will teach assembly newly written hymns.

8:15 p.m. Memorial Chapel	*SPRING ORCHESTRA CONCERT.* University Civic Orchestra. Conductor: Theo. Hoelty-Nickel. Soloists: William Kroeger, Newman Powell, William Walters. Reception at the Student Union after the concert

FRIDAY: April 19 8:00 a.m. Student Union	*REGISTRATION.* EXHIBITIONS.
8:45- 9:45 a.m. Gloria Christi Chapel	*JOINT SESSION*—Church Music Seminar and LSWMA. Dr. Theo. Hoelty-Nickel, Chairman.
	WORSHIP AND CONTEMPORARY MAN—I. Dr. Edgar S. Brown, Jr., Director of the Commission on Worship, Lutheran Church in America.
10:10-10:30 a.m.	*UNIVERSITY ASSEMBLY.* Speaker: Dr. Edgar S. Brown, Jr.
10:45-12:15 p.m. Memorial Chapel	*WORSHIP AND CONTEMPORARY MAN—II.* Professor Martin J. Naumann, Springfield, Illinois.
1:30- 2:30 p.m. Memorial Chapel Gallery	*ORGAN IMPROVISATION AND THE CHURCH SERVICE.* Demonstration and discussion. Professor Michael Schneider, Berlin; Professor Gregg Fountain, Northwestern University; Professor Philip Gehring, Valparaiso University; Professor Paul Manz, Concordia College, St. Paul, Minnesota.
3:00- 3:45 p.m. Student Union	*CONTEMPORARY CHURCH ARCHITECTURE.* Exhibition critique: Mr. Sewell J. Mathre, architect.
4:00- 5:00 p.m. Student Union Great Hall	*CONTEMPORARY ART IN THE CHURCH.* Religious film for Seattle World's Fair "Century 21" and examples from exhibition "Art for Religion." Moderator: The Rev. Donald Elder. Panel: Prof. Jim Crane, Wisconsin State College, Prof. John Maakestad, St. Olaf College. Mr. Charles Pohlmann, Sacred Design, Inc.
5:30 p.m. Student Union	Planning of year-round activities. Bring food from Cafeteria to meeting rooms designated on lounge announcement boards. Everyone welcome.
8:15 p.m. Memorial Chapel	*CONCERT.* Michael Schneider, Berlin, organist. Concordia Teachers College Choir, River Forest, Thomas Gieschen, conductor.
9:30 p.m.	*VESPERS.* Settings by Richard Wienhorst. Concordia Teachers College Choir. Speaker: M. J. Naumann; Herbert Gotsch, organist.
SATURDAY: April 20 8:00 a.m. Memorial Chapel	*REGISTRATION.* EXHIBITIONS.
8:45- 9:30 a.m. Memorial Chapel	*A SERVICE OF LESSONS AND CAROLS FOR EASTER WEEK.* A contemporary approach to a traditional English worship form. Robert Weinhold, officiant. University Students music

THE EDIFYING WORD

THE ORDER OF THE OPENING SERVICE
48TH REGULAR CONVENTION OF THE LUTHERAN CHURCH–MISSOURI SYNOD
RED ROCKS AMPHITHEATRE, MORRISON, COLORADO
JULY 11, 1969, 7:30 P.M.

PARTICIPANTS IN THE SERVICE

Officiant: THE REV. DR. GERHARD H. MUNDINGER

Lector: THE REV. WALDEMAR E. MEYER

Preacher: THE REV. DR. PAUL W. STREUFERT

Organist: DR. PAUL MANZ

Choirmaster: MR. GERHARD SCHROTH

The brass choir is from the Denver Symphony Orchestra. Singers are from the Lutheran churches of Denver. The Rodgers Organ Co. of Hillsboro, Oregon, is supplying a Model 990 instrument for use at this service and throughout the convention.

"Infant Holy, Infant Lowly" (W ZLOBIE LEZY)

"Twas in the Moon of Wintertime" (UNE JUENE PUCELLE)

"Bright and Glorious Is the Sky" (DEJLIG ER DEN HIMMEL BLAA)

"Were You There" (WERE YOU THERE),

"Hail Thee, Festival Day" (SALVE FESTA DIES)

"O Day Full of Grace" (DEN SIGNEDE DAG)

"We Who Once Were Dead" (MIDDEN IN DE DOOD)

"What Wondrous Love is This" (WONDROUS LOVE)

"The King of Love My Shepherd Is" (ST. COLUMBA)

"Praise, My Soul, the King of Heaven" (LAUDA ANIMA)

"Joyful, Joyful We Adore Thee" (HYMN TO JOY)

"Earth and All Stars" (EARTH AND ALL STARS)

"Oh, For a Thousand Tongues to Sing" (AZMON)

APPENDIX 18: *Una Sancta* Kyrie and Hymn of the Day

Cantor Kyrie, eleison.

Ch Kyrie, eleison.

A For godly judgment in this land:

C Lord, O Lord, have mer - cy.

A For a godly division of all of its goods:

C Lord, O Lord, have mer - cy.

A That good be the news to the poor, O pray to the Lord:

C Lord, O Lord, have mer - cy.

Help us, save us, com - fort, de - fend us,

gra - cious Lord! A - men.

1. We stood be - low the roll - ing moun - tain -
2. The proph - ets cried the con - se - quence of
3. We forged a cross, a sword thrust in the

smoke And trem-bled to be there, for there you spoke:
sin, That we would not be whole, as we had been.
earth, And with that cross killed him who yearned our birth;

Ah, thun - der, thun - der, Oh, the voice of God.
Ah, scat - ter, scat - ter At the voice of God.
Then curs - ing, curst, we Feared the wrath of God.

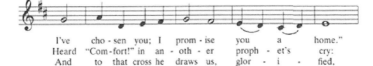

But you said, "Is - rael, you_____ are my own;
But we, who crept be - low an al - ien sky,
But see the cross: it lifts our Lord on high;

I've cho - sen you; I prom - ise you a home."
Heard "Com-fort!" in an - oth - er proph - et's cry:
And to that cross he draws us, glor - i - fied.

Then we— we roared be - fore your moun-tain - throne
"The Lord shall send his ser - vant from on high
Who, 'round that cross, with one voice mag - ni - fy

12

The won-der, won-der:	"Glo-ry to our God!"
To gath-er, gath-er	As a shep-herd should."
The mer-cy, mer-cy,	Oh, the grace of God!

THE NICENE CREED (spoken)

C We believe in one God,
the Father, the Almighty,
maker of heaven and earth,
of all that is, seen and unseen.
We believe in one Lord, Jesus Christ,
the only Son of God,
eternally begotten of the Father,
God from God, Light from Light,
true God from true God,
begotten, not made,
of one Being with the Father.
Through him all things were made.
For us and for our salvation
   he came down from heaven;
   by the power of the Holy Spirit
      he became incarnate from the virgin Mary, and was made man.
For our sake he was crucified under Pontius Pilate;
   he suffered death and was buried.
   On the third day he rose again
      in accordance with the Scriptures;
   he ascended into heaven
      and is seated at the right hand of the Father.
He will come again in glory to judge the living and the dead,
   and his kingdom will have no end.
We believe in the Holy Spirit, the Lord, the giver of life,
   who proceeds from the Father and the Son.
With the Father and the Son he is worshiped and glorified.
He has spoken through the prophets.
We believe in one holy catholic and apostolic Church.
We acknowledge one Baptism for the forgiveness of sins.
We look for the resurrection of the dead,
   and the life of the world to come. Amen

Sit
The offering is received.
THE OFFERTORY (sung by children's choir; congregation stand)

It is suggested that children of the congregation come forward bearing many and various thanksgiving gifts: the Communion elements, the plates, food, clothing, symbols

13

APPENDIX 19: Sing, My Tongue, The Glorious Battle hymn festival programs

HYMN FESTIVAL

St. Stephen Lutheran Church, Wausau, Wisconsin
April 15, 1988, 8:00 p.m.

"Sing My Tongue, The Glorious Battle"

Christ Jesus the Redeemer...

INTRODUCTION TO THE THEME and READING -- Philippians 2:5-11

HYMN - "Sing My Tongue"   *Fortunatus New*
    Lutheran Book of Worship #118
    1. all   2. women
    3. all   4. men
            5. all *(stand)*

READING - "The Glory of the Cross" - O. P. Krezmann

HYMN - "Jesus Christ is Risen Today"   *Easter Hymn*
    Lutheran Book of Worship #151
    1. all   2. women; men enter only on "Alleluia"
    3. men; women at "Alleluia"   4. all in unison

...Being Found in Human Form...

READING - St. John 1:1-14

HYMN - "All Hail to You, O Blessed Morn"   *Wie schön leuchtet*
    Lutheran Book of Worship # 73
    1. all   3. all in harmony (using Bach setting - insert)
    2. choir (using Bach setting)   4. all in unison *(stand)*

. . . He Humbled Himelf Unto Death on a Cross. . .

READING – "The Biography" – Thomas Merton

HYMN – "O Sacred Head Now Wounded"   *Herzlich Tut Mich Verlangen*
   Lutheran Book of Worship #117
    1. all   3. choir (using Bach setting)
    2. organ   4. all (using Bach setting – insert)

READING – "Free Grace" – Charles Wesley

HYMN – "Were You There?"   *Were You There*
   Lutheran Book of Worship # 92
    1. all   3. choir
    2. organ   4. all (in harmony)

. . . To Be Exalted By God the Father.

READING – "Easter Monday" – Christina Rosetti

HYMN – "Christ Jesus Lay in Death's Strong Bands"   *Christ Lag in Todesbanden*
   Lutheran Book of Worship #134
    1. all   3. choir (using Bach setting)
    2. organ   4. all
      5. all (using Bach setting-insert)

READING – "The Sting of Death" – Paul A. Washburn

HYMN – "Lo! He Comes With Clouds Descending"   *Helmsley*
   Lutheran Book of Worship #27
    1. all   2. choir; all join at "Deeply wailing"
    3. organ   4. all *(stand)*

OFFERING

PRAYERS and BENEDICTION

HYMN – "Now All the Vault of Heaven Resound"   *Lasst Uns Erfreuen*
        1. all
        2. women; men join at "Alleluia"
        3. men; women join at "Alleluia"
        4. all

POSTLUDE: Improvisation

****

Participants

JOHN SWENSEN, Senior Pastor, St. Stephen Lutheran Church
LINDA LOCKLIN, Intern Pastor, St. Andrew Lutheran Church
DONOVAN J. PALMQUIST, Vice President for Development, Lutheran School
    of Theology at Chicago
RANDALL R. LEE, Associate Vice President for Development, Lutheran School
    of Theology at Chicago
PAUL MANZ, Christ Seminary-Seminex Professor of Church Music and Artist
    in Residence, Lutheran School of Theology at Chicago
CHOIRS of the Lutheran Churches of Wausau, Darlene Johnson, Coordinator;
    Jim Lee, Director

Several benefactors have agreed to match gifts received at the Hymn Festival. An envelope has been enclosed in the program for your use. Please print *your name and address on the envelope so that we can thank you for your gift.*

You are cordially invited to a reception following the hymn festival in the Church Parlors.

HYMN FESTIVAL

Kountze Memorial Lutheran Church, Omaha, Nebraska
May 18, 1988, 7:30 p.m.

"Sing My Tongue, The Glorious Battle"

Christ Jesus the Redeemer...

INTRODUCTION TO THE THEME and READING -- Philippians 2:5-11

HYMN – "Sing My Tongue"   *Fortunatus New*
    Lutheran Book of Worship #118
    1. all   2. women
    3. all   4. men
        5. all *(stand)*

READING – "The Glory of the Cross" – O. P. Kreztmann

HYMN – "Love Divine All Loves Excelling"   *Hyfrydol*
    Lutheran Book of Worship #315
    1. choir   2. all
    3. all (in harmony)   4. all in unison

... Being Found in Human Form...

READING – St. John 1:1-14

HYMN – "A Stable Lamp is Lighted"   *Sittler*
    (see insert)
    1. choir women   3. choir men
    2. all   4. all

... He Humbled Himelf Unto Death on a Cross...

READING – "The Biography" – Thomas Merton

HYMN – "Were You There"   *Were You There*
    Lutheran Book of Worship #92
    1. all   3. choir
    2. organ   4. all (in harmony)

... To Be Exalted By God the Father...

READING – "Praise to the Holiest" – John Henry Cardinal Newman

HYMN – "Christ Jesus Lay in Death's Strong Bands"   *Christ Lag in Todesbanden*
    Lutheran Book of Worship # 134
    1. all   3. choir
    2. organ   4. all (in harmony, using Bach setting - insert)
        5. all in union (stand)

READING – "My Baptismal Birthday" – Samuel Taylor Coleridge

HYMN – "We Know That Christ is Raised"   *Engelberg*
    Lutheran Book of Worship #189
    1. all   3. men; women join at "Alleluia"
    2. women; men join at "Alleluia" 4. all

... And Confessed By Every Tongue.

READING – "Eternal Light" – Thomas Binney

HYMN – "O Holy Spirit, Brooding Dove"   *Tietjen*
    (see insert)
    1. all   2. men
    3. all   4. women
        5. all in unison

READING – "God's Grandeur" – Gerard Manley Hopkins

HYMN – "Come Share the Spirit"   *Come Share the Spirit*
    (see insert)
    1. choir
    2. women; men join at "Christ speaks..."
    3. men; women join at "Christ speaks..."
    4. all

OFFERING – "Come, Be Joyful, Raise a Shout" – David Johnson

PRAYERS and BENEDICTION

HYMN – "O Day Full of Grace"   *Den Sugnede Dag*
        1. all   2. men
        3. all   4. women
             5. all

POSTLUDE: Improvisation

****

Participants

LAWRENCE W. WICK, Senior Pastor, Kountze Memorial Lutheran Church
HAROLD E. SCHMIDT, Senior Pastor, First Lutheran Church
DONOVAN J. PALMQUIST, Vice President for Development, Lutheran School
    of Theology at Chicago
RANDALL R. LEE, Associate Vice President for Development, Lutheran School
    of Theology at Chicago
PAUL MANZ, Christ Seminary-Seminex Professor of Church Music and Artist
    in Residence, Lutheran School of Theology at Chicago
CHOIR of Kountze Memorial Lutheran Church, Mary Sayre, Director

*Several benefactors have agreed to match gifts received at the Hymn
Festival. An envelope has been enclosed in the program for your use.
Please* print *your name and address on the envelope so that we can
thank you for your gift.*

You are invited to a reception following the hymn festival in the Fellowship
Room of the Church.

APPENDIX 20: "Tomorrow Shall Be My Dancing Day" Hymn Festival Program

"Tomorrow Shall Be My Dancing Day"
A Hymn Festival Celebrating the Crucified Christ
St. Martin's Lutheran Church
Austin, Texas
9 March 1989

Prelude – "I Danced in the Morning"

Lord of the Dance

Refrain: All
1. women
2. all
3. choir
4. men
5. all

1. I danced in the
2. I danced for the
3. I danced on the
4. I danced on a
5. They cut me

mom-ing when the world was be-gun, And I danced in the
scribe and the phar-i-see, But they would-n't
Sab-bath and I cured the lame: The ho-ly peo-ple
Fri-day when the sky turned black; It's hard to
down and I leap up high; I am the

moon and the stars and the sun, And I
dance, and they would-n't fol-low me; I
said it was a shame. They
dance with the dev-il on your back. They
life that-'ll nev-er, nev-er die; I'll

2

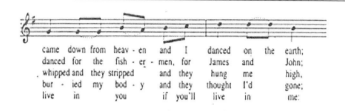

came down from heav - en and I danced on the earth;
danced for the fish - er - men, for James and John;
whipped and they stripped and they hung me high,
bur - ied my bod - y and they thought I'd gone;
live in you if you'll live in me:

At Beth - le - hem I had my birth.
They came with me and the dance went on.
And left me there on a cross to die.
But I am the dance and I still go on.
I am the Lord of the Dance, said he.

Dance then wher - ev - er you may be; I am the Lord of the

Dance, said he, And I'll lead you all, wher - ev - er you may be.

1.4.   1.5.

And I'll lead you all in the dance, said he.   dance, said he.

Introduction to the Theme

God Gives the Son for Us in Death

Reading – Romans 8:31–39

3

Hymn – "O Love, How Deep" *Deo Gracias*
　　Lutheran Book of Worship #88
　　　　1. all
　　　　2. women
　　　　3. all
　　　　4. men
　　　　5. all
　　　　6. organ
　　　　7. all *(stand)*

Reading – "You are Holy" from *Biblical Prayers* – Lucien Deiss
Hymn – "Peace Came to Earth" *Schneider*
　　　　1. women; men join at "Who could but sing;. . ."
　　　　2. all
　　　　3. men; women join at "Who could but thrill;. . ."
　　　　4. all

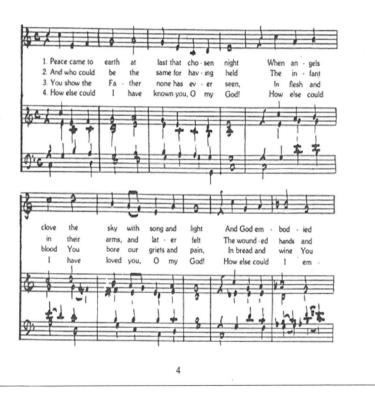

4

Offering

(Several generous donors have agreed to match the offering received at this evening's hymn festival. The offering will be used for Educational Grants at the Lutheran School of Theology at Chicago.)

Hymn "Tomorrow Shall Be My Dancing Day"   *My Dancing Day*

(see insert)

Refrain is sung by all

1. choir women
2. all women
3. all
6. women
9. all
10. men
11. all

Prayers *(stand)*

Benediction

Hymn – "Now All the Vault of Heaven Resounds"   *Lasst Uns Erfreuen*

Lutheran Book of Worship #143

1. all
2. women; men join at "Alleluia"
3. men; women join at "Alleluia"
4. all

Participants

The Rev. Dean W. Bard, Associate Vice President for Development, Lutheran School of Theology at Chicago

The Rev. Sharon Kelly, Associate Pastor, St. Mark's Lutheran Church

The Rev. Keith W. Klockau, Pastor, All Saints Lutheran Church, Kansas City, KS

The Rev. Dr. William E. Lesher, President, Lutheran School of Theology at Chicago

Dr. Paul Manz, Christ Seminary-Seminex Professor of Church Music and Artist in Residence, Lutheran School of Theology at Chicago; Cantor, the Evangelical Lutheran Church of Saint Luke, Chicago.

Mr. Reuben Reynolds, Organist-Choirmaster, St. Mark's Lutheran Church

The Rev. Timothy Swanson, Pastor, St. Mark's Lutheran Church

"Tomorrow Shall Be My Dancing Day"
A Hymn Festival Celebrating the Crucified and Risen Christ
St. John's Roman Catholic Church
Des Moines, Iowa
21 May 1989

Prelude – "I Danced in the Morning"   *Lord of the Dance*
    All hymns for tonight's Hymn Festival are printed in the insert.
        Refrain: all
        1. women
        2. all
        3. choir
        4. men
        5. all

Introduction to the Theme

God Gives the Son for Us in Death

    Reading – Romans 8:31-39
    Hymn – "All Glory Be to God on High"   *Allein Gott In Der Höh*

        1. all
        2. choir *(in harmony)*
        3. all *(in harmony)*
        4. all *(in unison)*

    Reading – "You are Holy" from *Biblical Prayers* – Lucien Deiss
    Hymn – "Peace Came to Earth"   *Schneider*

        1. women; men join at "Who could but sing…"
        2. all
        3. men; women join at "Who could but thrill…"
        4. all

God Raises Jesus from the Dead

    Reading – "Free Grace" – Charles Wesley
    Hymn – "Jesus Lives! The Victory's Won"   *Jesus, Meine Zuversicht*

        1. all
        2. women; men join at "This shall be…"
        3. all
        4. men; women join at "This shall be…"
        5. all

Reading – "What a Glorious Spectacle" from *The Church's Year of Grace* – Pius Parsch
Hymn – "Now the Green Blade Rises"   *Noël Nouvelet*

    1. choir
    2. women; men join at "Love is come again..."
    3. men; women join at "Love is come again..."
    4. all

Reading – "But the Christian" from *For the Life of the World* – Alexander Schmemann
Hymn – "Awake, My Heart, With Gladness"   *Auf, Auf, Mein Herz*

    1. all
    2. men
    3. all
    4. women
    5. organ
    6. all

Who Then Can Separate Us from God's Love?

Reading – from *Gravity and Grace* – Joseph Sittler
Hymn – "We Who Once Were Dead"   *Midden in De Dood*

    1. women
    2. men
    3. all
    4. organ
    5. choir
    6. all

Reading – "What Are" – Gregory the Great
Hymn – "The King of Love My Shepherd Is"   *St. Columba*

    1. all
    2. choir *(in harmony)*
    3. all *(in harmony)*
    4. choir in canon
    5. all in canon; men begin with the organ, women enter one measure later
    6. all

Reading – from "The Sting of Death" – Paul Washburn
Hymn – "Lord, Thee I Love With All My Heart"   *Herzlich Lieb*

    1 - 3. all

Greeting

Offering

(Several generous donors have agreed to match the offering received at this evening's hymn festival. The offering will be used for Educational Grants at the Lutheran School of Theology at Chicago.)

Hymn "Tomorrow Shall Be My Dancing Day" *My Dancing Day*

Refrain is sung by all
1. choir women
2. all women
3. all
6. women
9. all
10. men
11. all

Prayers *(stand)*

Benediction

Hymn – "O Day Full of Grace" *Den Signede Dag*

1. all
2. women
3. all
4. men
5. all

Participants

The Rev. Paul R. Axness, Campus Pastor, Grand View College, Des Moines
The Rev. Dean W. Bard, Associate Vice President for Development, Lutheran School of Theology at Chicago
The Rev. Robert D. Dotzel, Pastor, St. John's Lutheran Church, Des Moines
The Rev. Gregory Nelson Davis, Pastor, St. James Lutheran Church, Johnston, Iowa
The Rev. Randall R. Lee, Associate Vice President for Development, Lutheran School of Theology at Chicago
Dr. Paul Manz, Christ Seminary-Seminex Professor of Church Music and Artist in Residence, Lutheran School of Theology at Chicago; Cantor, the Evangelical Lutheran Church of Saint Luke, Chicago
Choir: Musica Ecclesia, Dr. Aimee Beckmann-Collier, director

"So Much to Sing About"

A Hymn Festival for the Celebration of Advent
Christ Church Cathedral
St. Louis
8 December 1989

Prelude   *In dir ist Freude*   J.S. Bach

Creation's Song

Reading   Isaiah 35: 1–10
Hymn   "Prepare the Way, O Zion"   *Bereden Väg För Herran*
              Hymnal 1982 #65
                    Refrain: all
                    1. women
                    2. men
                    3. all *(stand)*

Reading   "Have Ye Not Known?" - Anonymous
Hymn   "Hark the Glad Sound!"   *Richmond*
              Hymnal 1982 #72
                    1. all
                    2. men
                    3. women
                    4. all

Mary's Song

Reading   "Continuing the Incarnation" - St. John of the Cross
Hymn   "The Angel Gabriel"   *Gabriel's Message*
              Hymnal 1982 #265
                    1. choir *(in harmony)*
                    2. women
                    3. men
                    4. all *(in harmony)*

Reading   "Sing We A Song of High Revolt" - Fred Kaan
Hymn   "Tell Out My Soul"   *Woodlands*
              Hymnal 1982 #438
                    1. choir men
                    2. all
                    3. choir women
                    4. all *(stand)*

The Angels' Song

Reading	"The Incarnation" - Charles Wesley	
Hymn	"Angels We Have Heard on High"	*Gloria*
	Hymnal 1982 #96	

Refrain: all *(in harmony)*
1. all
2. choir *(in harmony)*
3. women
4. all *(in harmony)*

Reading	from: "Upon the Midnight Clear" - O.P. Kretzmann	
Hymn	"While Shepherds Watched Their Flocks"	*Winchester Old*
	Hymnal 1982 #94	

1. all
2. choir *(in harmony)*
3. all *(in harmony)*
4. women; men join at "all meanly wrapped..."
5. men; women join at "of angels praising..."
6. all *(stand)*

Our Song

Reading	from A Christmas Homily - Leo the Great	
Hymn	"Break Forth, O Beauteous Heavenly Light"	*Ermuntre dich*
	Hymnal 1982 #91	

1. all *(in harmony) (stand)*

Reading	"Christ is Born" from Seasons of Celebration - Thomas Merton	
Hymn	"Of the Father's Love Begotten"	*Divinum Mysterium*
	Hymnal 1982 #82	

1. choir
2. men
3. women
4. all *(stand)*

Homily	The Rev. Dr. John H. Tietjen

Hymn	"So Much to Sing About"	*Manz*

1. choir
2. women
3. men
4. all

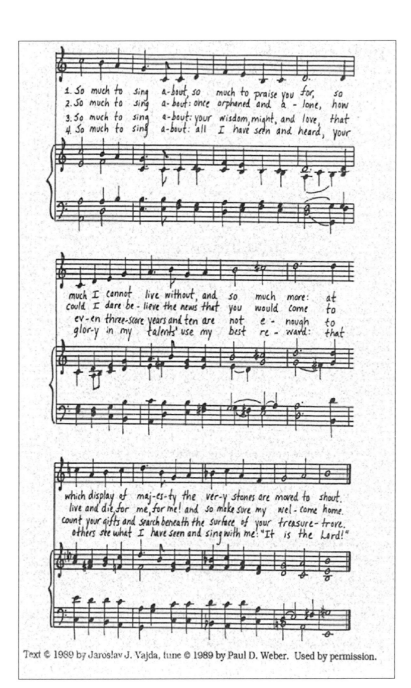

1. So much to sing a-bout, so much to praise you for, so
2. So much to sing a-bout: once orphaned and a - lone, how
3. So much to sing a-bout: your wisdom, might, and love, that
4. So much to sing a-bout: all I have seen and heard, your

much I cannot live without, and so much more: at
could I dare be - lieve the news that you would come to
ev - en three-score years and ten are not e - nough to
glor-y in my talents' use my best re - ward: that

which display of maj-es-ty the ver-y stones are moved to shout.
live and die for me, for me! and so make sure my wel-come home.
count your gifts and search beneath the surface of your treasure-trove.
others see what I have seen and sing with me: "It is the Lord!"

Text © 1989 by Jaroslav J. Vajda, tune © 1989 by Paul D. Weber. Used by permission.

Greeting   The Rev. Dr. William E. Lesher

Offering   Choir Anthems:
               "Zion, at Thy Shining Gates"   George Guest
               "Stir Up, Lord, Your Power"   Haya tune
                                                          Text: Mark P. Bangert
               "E'en So, Lord Jesus, Quickly Come"   Paul Manz

Prayers *(stand)*

Benediction

Hymn   "Christians Awake"   *Yorkshire*
               Hymnal 1982 #106
                    1. choir
                    2. all
                    3. men; women join at "peace on earth..."
                    4. women; men join at "the earliest heralds..."
                    5. choir
                    6. all

Participants

The Rev. Dr. Mark P. Bangert, Christ Seminary-Seminex Professor of Worship and Music
   Lutheran School of Theology at Chicago
The Rev. Dennis R. Hallemeier, Assistant to the Bishop, Missouri-Kansas Synod
   St. Louis
Mrs. Betty Hecht, Trinity Lutheran Church
   Manchester
The Rev. Dr. William E. Lesher, President
   Lutheran School of Theology at Chicago
The Rev. Gerald L. Mansholt, Pastor, Living Christ Lutheran Church
   Florissant
Dr. Paul Manz, Christ Seminary-Seminex Professor of Church Music and Artist in Residence
   Lutheran School of Theology at Chicago
   Cantor, the Evangelical Lutheran Church of Saint Luke, Chicago.
The Rev. Dr. Larry W. Neeb, Creative Communications for the Parish, Inc.
   St. Louis
Seminarian Jane Ralph Rehwaldt, Zion Lutheran Church
   Ferguson
The Rev. Dr. John H. Tietjen, Pastor, Trinity Lutheran Church
   Fort Worth, TX
   Former President, Christ Seminary-Seminex

Appreciation is extended to Mr. Kim Kolander, Choir Director of Gethsemane Lutheran Church,
St. Louis, MO, who led the Festival Choir in preparation for this service.

The Hymn Festival was designed by the Rev. Randall R. Lee, Chicago.

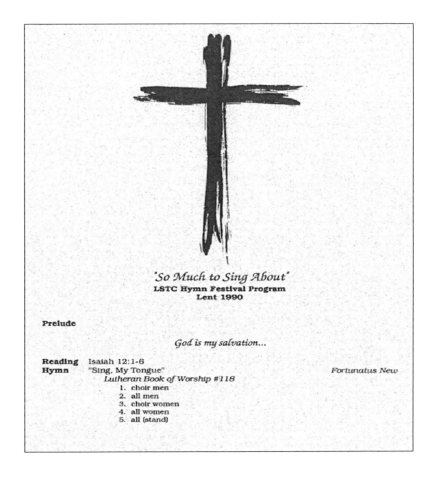

"*So Much to Sing About*"
LSTC Hymn Festival Program
Lent 1990

Prelude

God is my salvation...

Reading   Isaiah 12:1-6
Hymn   "Sing, My Tongue"   *Fortunatus New*
     Lutheran Book of Worship #118
         1. choir men
         2. all men
         3. choir women
         4. all women
         5. all (stand)

Reading "Weary of all Trumpeting" – Martin Franzmann
Hymn "Hail Thou Once Despised Jesus"   *In Bablione*
          Hymnal 1982 #495
            1. all
            2. women; men join at "All thy people..."
            3. men; women join at "There for sinners..."
            4. all

Reading   "The Passion and Exaltation of Christ" — Isaac Watts
Hymn   "Glory Be to Jesus"   *Wem in Leidenstagen*
          Hymnal 1982 #479

1. all
2. women
3. organ
4. men
5. all *(stand)*

1 Glo - ry be to Je - sus, who in bit - ter pains
2 Grace and life e - ter - nal in that blood I find,
3 Blest through end - less a - ges be the pre - cious stream
4 Oft as earth ex - ult - ing wafts its praise on high,
5 Lift ye then your voic - es; swell the might - y flood;

1 poured for me the life - blood from his sa - cred veins!
2 blest be his com - pas - sion in - fi - nite - ly kind!
3 which from sin and sor - row doth the world re - deem!
4 an - gel hosts re - joic - ing, make their glad re - ply.
5 loud - er still and loud - er praise the pre - cious blood.

3

...my Strength and my Song

Reading   "Praise to the Holiest" – John Henry Cardinal Newman
Hymn   "I'll Praise My Maker"   *Old 113th*
               Hymnal 1982 #429
                   1. choir
                   2. women; men join at "whose truth forever..."
                   3. men; women join at "He helps the stranger..."
                   4. all *(stand)*

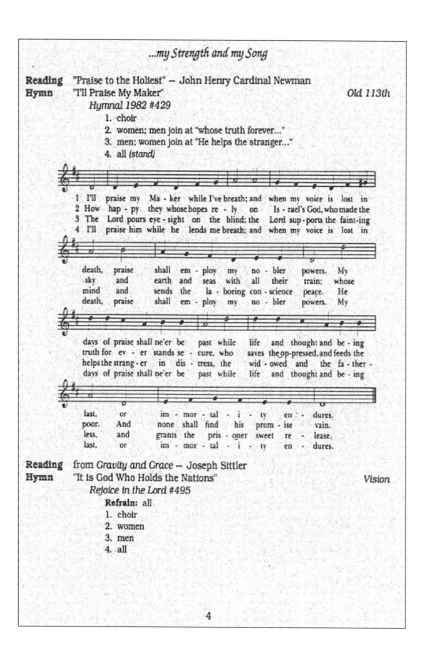

Reading   from *Gravity and Grace* – Joseph Sittler
Hymn   "It is God Who Holds the Nations"   *Vision*
               Rejoice in the Lord #495
                   Refrain: all
                   1. choir
                   2. women
                   3. men
                   4. all

4

1. It is God who holds the na-tions in the hol-low of his hand;
2. It is God whose pur-pose sum-mons us to use the pres - ent hour,
* 3. When a thank-ful na-tion, look-ing back, u - nites to cel - e - brate
4. He re - minds us ev - ery sun-rise that the earth is ours on lease—

1. it is God whose light is shin-ing in the dark-ness of the land;
2. who re - calls us to our sens-es when a na-tion's life turns sour;
3. those who win our ad - mi - ra-tion by their ser-vice to the state,
4. for the sake of life to - mor-row may our love for it in - crease;

1. it is God who builds his Cit - y on the Rock and not on sand:
2. in the dis - ci - pline of free-dom we shall know his sav-ing power:
3. when self - giv - ing is a mea-sure of the great - ness of the great,
4. may all rac - es live to - geth - er, share its rich - es, be at peace:

Refrain: (God be praised!.....)

1. may the liv - ing God be praised! _____
2. may the liv - ing God be praised! _____
3. may the liv - ing God be praised! _____
4. may the liv - ing God be praised! _____

Reading   "You, O Christ" – Simeon the New Theologian
Hymn   "If God Himself Be For Me"   *Ist Gott Für Mich*
       Lutheran Book of Worship #454
              1. all
              2. men; women join at "without him..."
              3. women; men join at "but be destroyed..."
              4. all

5

Sing God's Praises Forever!

Reading from *Meditations on the Way of the Cross* — Brother Roger of Taizé
Hymn "Shout for Joy, Loud and Long!" *Personet Hodie*
Worship III #540
Refrain: all
1. choir
2. women
3. men
4. all *(stand)*

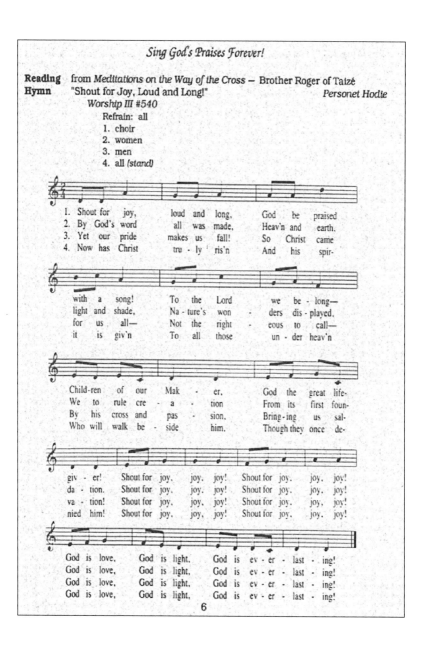

1. Shout for joy, loud and long, God be praised
2. By God's word all was made, Heav'n and earth.
3. Yet our pride makes us fall! So Christ came
4. Now has Christ tru - ly ris'n And his spir-

with a song! To the Lord we be - long—
light and shade, Na - ture's won - ders dis - played.
for us all— Not the right - eous to call—
it is giv'n To all those un - der heav'n

Child-ren of our Mak - er. God the great life-
We to rule cre - a - tion From its first foun-
By his cross and pas - sion. Bring-ing us sal-
Who will walk be - side him. Though they once de-

giv - er! Shout for joy, joy. joy! Shout for joy, joy, joy!
da - tion. Shout for joy, joy. joy! Shout for joy, joy, joy!
va - tion! Shout for joy, joy, joy! Shout for joy, joy, joy!
nied him! Shout for joy, joy, joy! Shout for joy, joy, joy!

God is love, God is light, God is ev - er - last - ing!
God is love, God is light, God is ev - er - last - ing!
God is love, God is light, God is ev - er - last - ing!
God is love, God is light, God is ev - er - last - ing!

6

Reading   "Sanctuary at Midnight" from *The Pilgrim* — O.P. Kretzmann

Hymn   "Blessing and Honor"   *American Hymn*
           Lutheran Book of Worship #525
             1. all
             2. men
             3. women
             4. all *(stand)*

Greeting

Offering   music to be determined

Hymn   "So Much to Sing About"   *Manz*
             1. choir   3. men
             2. women   4. all

Prayers *(Stand)*

Benediction

Hymn   "My Song is Love Unknown"   *Love Unknown*
            Christians Awake! #E-1
                    1. women
                    2. men
                    3. all

1. My song is love un - known, My Sav-ior's love for
2. He came from his blest throne, Sal - va - tion to be -
3. Here might I stay and sing, No sto - ry so di -

me, Love to the love-less shown That they might love - ly
stow, But all made strange, and none The longed-for Christ would
vine: Nev - er was love, dear King, Nev - er was grief like

be. Oh, who am I that for my sake My
know. But O my friend, my friend in - deed, Who
thine. This is my friend, in whose sweet praise I

Lord shall take frail flesh, and die.
at my need his life did spend.
all my days could glad - ly spend.

A FESTIVAL of the RESURRECTION
"Crown Him the Lord of Years"
The Resurrection and Aging
April 16, 1993

The poet and hymnwriter, Matthew Bridges, bears witness to the resurrection of the Crucified Christ by drawing attention to the One who created the universe and all that exists by naming him the redeemer, the potentate of time, who now reigns "ineffably sublime." Resurrection casts all creation into a different light, and similarly suggests that the end of life as we experience it on earth is transformed by the powerful promise of life everlasting.

As we prepare to enter the 21st century, we are bombarded by an ever-rapidly changing world scene. The geopolitical changes that surround us pale, however, in the face of medical advances that not only add to a spiraling national debt, but also hold out the promise for a longer and more fulfilling life. We are not long from the days when average life expectancy will soon reach the fourscore years of strength envisioned by the psalmist. Indeed, it seems that only the natural endurance qualities of the human body can bring this advance to a halt.

But with these blessings of a longer life lived more healthfully and productively there comes the burden of caring for an increasingly aging population. Before the middle of the next century there will be more aged and infirm people living in this country than able-bodied people to care for them.

Clearly our culture struggles with these opportunities, and with the challenges arising from an aging population. With advances in age come new challenges for the health care industry as people live for more than twenty years in what was once called the twilight of life. A new administration in Washington searches for the right formula for capping the spiraling health care costs associated with an older population. Numerous industries make it possible for people to work later in life, but in doing so often shut out graduating students desiring to enter the work force. New opportunities for vocations dedicated to serving older citizens will change the landscape of higher education institutions. Family life will change as well, as the nuclear family once again includes those of several generations and as the roles of parents and children are more frequently exchanged during people's lifetimes. And equally fascinating - and daunting - is the opportunity placed before the Church which now must minister to people in a variety of new settings, for longer periods of time.

How does our culture
and how does our soci
implications of an ag
Church best address th
creation in this changin
this good news place o
society? What is the
supporting all those or
What are the unique
family in promoting w
and for all generation
minister to the needs no
charged with their ca
Church, community, a
good of all concerned?
its ministers and other
try?

These questions ar
discussion at the 1993
purpose of our time tog
of a new age of ministr
places before us in mi
families. In worship,
study, and in music, w
gift of new life, even
sharing the power of re

We invite you to
Lord Jesus Christ with
ment and energy, give
and life-giving Spirit,
Lord of years."

S
Frida
8:45 a.m.   Registrati

9:00 a.m.   Morning

9:45 a.m.   "The Res
            Cultural
            Societal
   Dr. Melvin K
   Professor of Pr
   Director of Pro
   Luther Northw

10:45 a.m. "The Res
            Theologi
            Gospel In
   Dr. Melvin K

d these present changes
 cope with the many
 tion? How does the
 s of God's love for all
 What obligations does
 , and through them, on
ole of the Church in
ing makes an impact?
e community and the
d health for the aging
 can the Church best
der people, but to those
are the best ways for
o work together for the
ld the Church prepare
this new age of minis-

ill be the focus of our
the Resurrection. The
capture the excitement
ept the invitation God
o the elderly and their
ent, in fellowship, in
brate God's marvelous
etch new avenues for
 in a changing world.
e Resurrection of our
ugh renewed commit-
wer of God's holy-ing
led to "Crown him the

LE
, 1993

th Paschal Blessing

 and Aging:
ndings and
ns"

logy & Ministry
ging
inary

and Aging:
lations and
s"

11:45 a.m.   The Holy Eucharist

The Rev. David G. Abrahamson
Presiding Minister
The Rev. Dr. William Hughes, Preacher
Lutheran Home & Service for the Aged
Dr. Paul Manz, Organist

1:00 p.m.   Lunch

2:00 p.m.   "The Resurrection and Aging:
Community Concerns and
Social Support"
Ms. Marie Payes
Director, Lutheran Community Services
Arlington Heights, Illinois

3:15 p.m.   "The Resurrection and Aging: Family
Function and Home Wholeness"
The Rev. Karl Lutze
Executive Director, Association of Lutheran
Older Adults, Valparaiso, Indiana

4:15 p.m.   "The Resurrection and Aging: The
Church, Alpha & Omega...
Ending and Beginning"
Panel Discussion with **Dr. Melvin Kimble**
and
The Rev. Philip Anderson
Bereavement Director, Vitas Hospice Care
Homewood, Illinois
Dr. Marybeth Buschmann
Gerontological Researcher, University of
Illinois, Chicago, Illinois
Ms. Ruth Manz
Hospice Trainer and Volunteer

5:30 p.m.   Evening Prayer

6:15 p.m.   Social Hour and Dinner

8:00 p.m.   "Crown Him the Lord of Years"
The Resurrection and Aging.
Hymns for the Second Half of Life"
Organist: **Dr. Paul Manz**

Choir: *The Liturgical Choir of the*
Lutheran School of Theology at Chicago,
under the direction of
Dr. Mark Bangert

A Hymn Festival

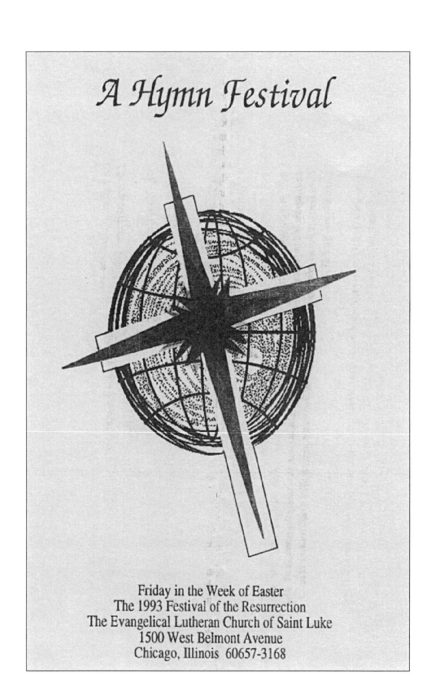

Friday in the Week of Easter
The 1993 Festival of the Resurrection
The Evangelical Lutheran Church of Saint Luke
1500 West Belmont Avenue
Chicago, Illinois 60657-3168

Crown Him the Lord of Years
The Resurrection and Aging.
Hymns for the Second Half of Life

Friday in the Week of Easter
April 16, 1993
8:00 p.m.

Music Before the Service
    Aria   ...Jan-Batiste Loellet
    Canzona   ...Filip De Monte

Hymn - "Now All the Vault of Heaven Resounds"   *Lasst Uns Erfreuen*
    Lutheran Book of Worship #143
              1. all
              2. men; women join at the final "Alleluia"
              3. women; men join at the final "Alleluia"
              4. all

Invocation

Sentences - P: Alleluia! Christ is Risen! Alleluia!
             C: He is Risen Indeed! Alleluia! Alleluia!
             P: The right hand of the Lord has done wonders!
             C: God's right hand has raised us up!
             P: I shall not die, I shall live!
             C: I shall proclaim what God has done!
             P: The stone which the builders had rejected
             C: Has now become the cornerstone.
             P: This is the work of God
             C: And wonderful in our eyes!
             P: Alleluia! Our hope is in him! Alleluia!
             C: He will take us into glory! Alleluia! Alleluia!

Prayer
    P: The Lord be with you.
    C: And also with you.
    P: Let us pray. Almighty God, you brighten this season with the glory of
        the resurrection. Keep us, your family, in the love of Christ. Renew
        us in body and soul, that our whole lives may be devoted to your
        service, through Jesus Christ, your Son, our Lord.
    C: Amen. *(Then the people sit)*

1

Crown Him the Lord of Years

Hope for the Years

Reading - "Spring has now Unwrapped the Flowers"   *16th Century Carol*

Hymn - "Be Happy, Saints"   *Arlington Heights*
    Be Happy, Saints #1
        1. all   4. men
        2. women   5. all
        3. all

Dwelling Secure

Reading - "It is the Small Things"   Anne Sexton

Hymn - "Praise My Soul the King of Heaven"   *Praise My Soul*
    Lutheran Book of Worship #549
        1. all   3. choir
        2. women   4. all

Endless Years

Reading - "Lord God, Your Love"   Brian Wren

Hymn - "God of the Ages"   *St. Catherine*
    (pg. 4)

        1. all   3. all, in harmony
        2. choir   4. all in unison

In Your Sight

Reading - "The Wise are Servants"   Romanos

Hymn - "How Can I Keep from Singing"   *Quaker Hymn*
    (pg. 5)

    All on the Refrain, "No storm can shake..."
        1. choir women   4. men
        2. women   5. all
        3. choir men

Borne Away

Reading - from *Gravity and Grace*   Joseph Sittler

Hymn - "Lord of Our Dawning"   *Dawning*
    Be Happy, Saints! #11

        1. choir women   4. men
        2. women   5. all
        3. choir men

2

Eternal Home

Reading - "The Heavenly City"   Gerard Manley Hopkins

Hymn - "O Morning Star, How Fair and Bright"   *Wie Schön Leuchtet*
    Lutheran Book of Worship #76
    1. all
    2 women, men join at "Now, though daily..."
    3. all
    4. men
    5. organ
    6. all (stand)

O God...

Reading - from *The Way of the Cross*   Mother Theresa of Calcutta and
                                                 Brother Roger of Taizé

Hymn - "O God Our Help in Ages Past"   *St. Anne*
    Lutheran Book of Worship #320
      A free improvisation will precede each stanza
      1. all   4. all, in harmony
      2. men   5. women
      3. choir   6. all (stand)

Offering
    (During the offering, the choir sings "Make Songs of Joy" in a setting by
    S. Drummond Wolf. The offering is received for the work of the
    Lutheran School of Theology at Chicago.)

Prayers
    (The people stand for the prayers and for the final hymn.)

    The Prayer for the Resurrection of our Lord
    The Prayer for the Festival
    The Prayer at Evening
    The Lord's Prayer

Benediction

Hymn - "Crown Him with many Crowns"   *Diademeta*
    Lutheran Book of Worship #170
      1. all   4. men
      2. choir   5. women
      3. all   6. all

3

"God of the Ages"

1. God of the a - ges, now and past, thank-ful of heart, we
2. God of our par - ents, teach-ers, friends, you gave them grace to
3. God of the pres - ent, guide us now; send us your Spir - it's
4. God of the fu - ture, grant us faith, cour-age for ven - tures

turn to you. God of the faith - ful year by year,
walk your way. May we, like them, a - rise to meet
ho - ly flame. Act-ing in cour - age, speak-ing love,
yet un - known. God, to the church your love has built

grant us your mer - cies ev - er new.
chal-leng-es, risks of our new day.
may we bring hon - or to your name. God of the a - ges,
now to their la - bors add our own.

hear our prayer; all gen - er - a - tions know your care.

4

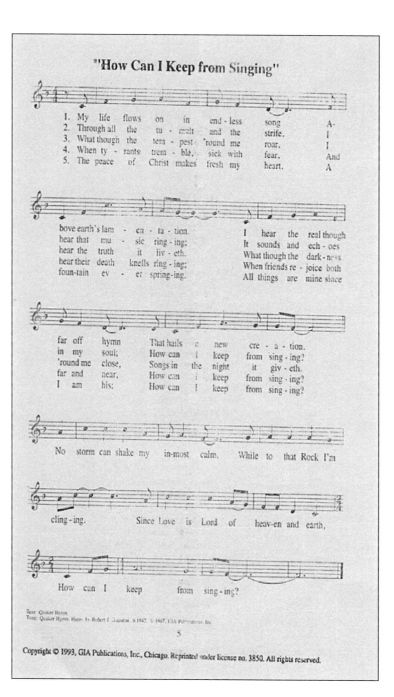

"How Can I Keep from Singing"

1. My life flows on in end - less song A-
2. Through all the tu - mult and the strife, I
3. What though the tem - pest 'round me roar, I
4. When ty - rants trem - ble, sick with fear, And
5. The peace of Christ makes fresh my heart, A

bove earth's lam - en - ta - tion, I hear the real though
hear that mu - sic ring - ing; It sounds and ech - oes
hear the truth it liv - eth. What though the dark - ness
hear their death knells ring - ing; When friends re - joice both
foun - tain ev - er spring - ing. All things are mine since

far off hymn That hails a new cre - a - tion.
in my soul; How can i keep from sing - ing?
'round me close, Songs in the night it giv - eth.
far and near, How can i keep from sing - ing?
I am his; How can I keep from sing - ing?

No storm can shake my in-most calm, While to that Rock I'm

cling - ing. Since Love is Lord of heav-en and earth,

How can I keep from sing - ing?

Text: Quaker Hymn
Tune: Quaker Hymn; Harm. by Robert J. Batastini, b.1942, © 1987, GIA Publications, Inc.

5

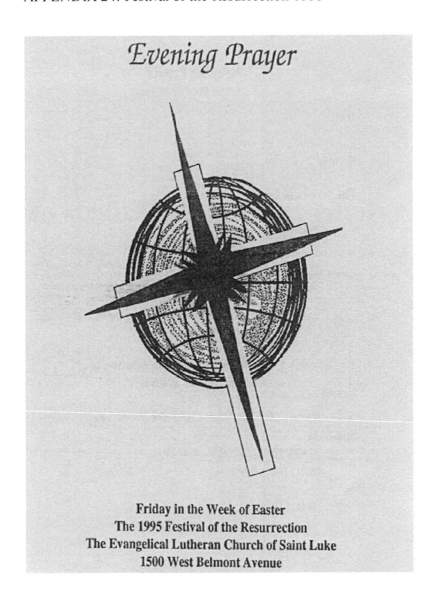

Evening Prayer

**Friday in the Week of Easter
The 1995 Festival of the Resurrection
The Evangelical Lutheran Church of Saint Luke
1500 West Belmont Avenue**

Evening Prayer
Lutheran Book of Worship
page 142

Prelude

The Service of Light

Versicles

L: Jesus Christ is risen from the dead.
C: Alleluia, alleluia, allelúia.

L: We are illumined by the brightness of his rising.
C: Alleluia, alleluia, allelúia.

L: Death has no more dominion over us.
C: Alleluia, alleluia, allelúia.

Hymn – "O Light Whose Splendor Thrills" #728

Psalmody
Thanksgiving for Light *(page 144)*

Psalm 141 *(pages 145-146)*

Psalm Prayer

Psalm 103

Psalm Prayer

Psalm 67

Psalm Prayer

Office Hymn – "Christ, Mighty Savior" #729

Lesson – II Corinthians 4:7-18

Response to the Lesson - "Erschienen ist der Herrlicher Tag"
...Schein

Gospel Canticle – "My Soul Proclaims Your Greatness" #730

Litany *(pages 148-151)*

Prayer for Peace *(page 151)*

Lord's Prayer *(Ecumenical Text, page 152)*

Benedicamus

Benediction

Officiant: The Rev. Randall R. Lee
              Grace Lutheran Church, Evanston, IL

Organist: James Freese, Organist
              Mount Calvary Lutheran Church, Milwaukee, WI

Choir: Altherbest Musicke, Bonnie Tipton Long, director
              The Church of Saint Luke, Chicago, IL

A Hymn Festival

Friday in the Week of Easter
The 1995 Festival of the Resurrection
The Evangelical Lutheran Church of Saint Luke
1500 West Belmont Avenue
Chicago, Illinois 60657-3168

"Life Together"
An Easter Hymn Festival
Celebrating the Life and Ministry of
Dietrich Bonhöffer
1906-1945

Prelude

Anthem "Alleluia Canon"   *Mozart Alleluia*

Hymn - "This Joyful Eastertide"(*With One Voicee*) #676   *Vruechten*
       Stanza 1 - women; men join at the Refrain
       Stanza 2 - men; women join at the Refrain
       Stanza 3 - all, rise

Invocation

Sentences

    L: Alleluia! Christ is risen!
    C: He is risen indeed! Alleluia!
    L: Here are words you may trust.
       Remember Jesus Christ, risen from the dead:
    C: He is our salvation, our eternal glory.
    L: If we die with him, we shall live with him:
    C: If we endure we shall reign with him.
    L: If we deny him, he will deny us:
    C: If we are faithless, he keeps faith.
    L: For he has broken the power of death:
    C: And brought life and immortality to light through the Gospel.

Prayer

    L: The Lord be with you.
    C: And also with you.,
    L: Let us pray. God of mercy, we no longer look for Jesus among
       the dead, for he is alive and has become the Lord of life. From
       the waters of death you raise us with him and renew your gift of
       life within us. Increase in our minds and hearts the risen life we
       share with Christ, and help us to grow as your people toward
       the fullness of eternal life with you, through Christ our Lord,
       who lives and reigns with you and the Holy Spirit, one God,
       now and forever.
    C: Amen.

Life Together: Through and In Jesus Christ

Introduction

Reading - from *The Cost of Discipleship*
Hymn – "Here in This Place" #718   *Gather Us In*
>   *Stanza 1 - choir*   *Stanza 3 - men*
>   *Stanza 2 - women*   *Stanza 4 - all*

Life Together: By Water and the Spirit

Reading - from a baptismal sermon by Bonhöffer in prison
Hymn – "Oh, Blessed Spring" #695   *Bergland*
>   *Stanza 1 - choir*   *Stanza 4 - men*
>   *Stanza 2 - women*   *Stanza 5- all*
>   *Stanza 3 - all*

Life Together: Praying the Scriptures

Reading - from *Life Together*
Hymn – "We Are All One in Mission" #755   *Kourtane*
>   *Stanza 1 - women; men join at "A single great commission..."*
>   *Stanza 2 - men; women join at "to touch the lives of others..."*
>   *Stanza 3 - all*

Life Together: Singing the New Song

Reading - from *Life Together*
Hymn – "Oh, Sing to the Lord" #795   *Cantad al Señor*
>   *Stanza 1 - choir*   *Stanza 4 - men*
>   *Stanza 2 - women*   *Stanza 5- all in Spanish*
>   *Stanza 3 - all in Spanish*

Life Together: Fellowship at the Table

Reading - from *Life Together*
Hymn – "Draw Us in the Spirit's Tether" #703   *Union Seminary*
>   *Stanza 1 - women; men join at "Alleluia!"*
>   *Stanza 2 - men; women join at "Alleluia!"*
>   *Stanza 3 - all*

Life Together: The Ministry of Proclaiming

Reading - from *Ethics*
Hymn – "Christ is Arisen! Alleluia! #678   *Mfurahini, Haleluya*
    Stanza 1 - all   Stanza 4 - choir in harmony
    Stanza 2 - women   Stanza 5 - all in harmony
    Stanza 3 - men

Life Together: The Ministry of Bearing

Reading - from *The Cost of Discipleship*
Hymn – "By Gracious Powers" #736   *Berlin*
    Stanza 1 - choir   Stanza 4 - men
    Stanza 2 - women   Stanza 5 - all
    Stanza 3 - all

Life Together: The Communion of Saints

Reading - from *Letters and Papers from Prison*
Hymn – "Rejoice in God's Saints" #689   *Laudate Dominum*
    Stanza 1 - all
    Stanza 2 - men; women join at "some carry the Gospel..."
    Stanza 3 - women; men join at "they share our complaining.."
    Stanza 4 - all

Life Together: The Kingdom of God

Reading - from *Letters and Papers from Prison*
Hymn – "My Lord, What a Morning" #627   *Burleigh*
    Refrain: all in harmony
    Stanza 1 - choir   Stanza 3 - men
    Stanza 2 - women

Offering

Voluntary

Prayers

Blessing

Hymn – "Alleluia! Jesus is Risen!" #674   *Earth and All Stars*
    Refrain: all
    Stanza 1 - all   Stanza 4 - women
    Stanza 2 - men   Stanza 5 - all
    Stanza 3 - all

APPENDIX 25: *With One Voice* Hymns

"All My Hope in God is Founded" (MICHAEL)

"Alleluia! Jesus is Risen!" (EARTH AND ALL STARS)

"Alleluia, Song of Gladness" (PRAISE, MY SOUL)

"Awake, Awake, and Greet the New Morn" (REJOICE, REJOICE)

"Be Thou My Vision" (SLANE)

"Before the Marvel of this Night" (MARVEL)

"Cantad al Señor" (CANTAD AL SEÑOR)

"Christ is Made the Sure Foundation" (WESTMINSTER ABBEY)

"Gift of Finest Wheat" (BICENTENNIAL)

"How Can I Keep from Singing"
   (HOW CAN I KEEP FROM SINGING)

"I Am the Bread of Life" (I AM THE BREAD)

"I Want to Walk As a Child of the Light" (HOUSTON)

"Jesu, Jesu, Fill Us with Your Love" (CHERAPONI)

"My Life Flows On in Endless Song"
   (HOW CAN I KEEP FROM SINGING)

"Peace Came to Earth" (SCHNEIDER)

"Shout for Joy Loud and Long" (PERSONENT HODIE)

"When in Our Music God is Glorified" (ENGELBERG)

APPENDIX 26: "Jesus Christ, My Sure Defense"

A FESTIVAL OF GREAT HYMNS

Paul Manz, Organist

October 29, 1980
7:30 p.m.

Sponsored by
University Christian Church
In Celebration of the Fiftieth Anniversary
of The Fort Worth Chapter, American Guild of Organists

DR. PAUL MANZ

Paul Manz is Cantor of Mount Olive Lutheran Church, Minneapolis, Minnesota. This position extends his ministry past the bounds of his local parish (where he remains as minister of music) enabling him to serve the whole church as composer, recitalist, teacher, lecturer and leader in worship. Under the auspices of this call, he is currently serving Gustavus Adolphus College, St. Peter, Minnesota, as adjunct professor. He is also associated with Luther Seminary, St. Paul, Minnesota, serves as a visiting professor at Christ Seminary-Seminex in St. Louis, Missouri, and as a consultant to the Music Department at Augsburg College, Minneapolis, Minnesota.

A native of Cleveland, Ohio, Paul Manz received his graduate degree from Northwestern University, Evanston, Illinois. He studied on a Fulbright grant at the Royal Flemish Conservatory in Antwerp with Flor Peeters. While in Europe he also studied with Helmut Walcha.

Dr. Manz has concertized extensively in North America. His hymn festivals have been warmly received throughout the nation, and as one reviewer defined them, they are "religious-musical experiences" of the highest order.

INSTRUCTIONS FOR CONGREGATION

The hymns are to be sung as follows:

U — All voices in unison
H — All voices in harmony
M — Men's voices in unison
W — Women's voices in unison
Ch — Choir voices only
O — Organ only

Spoken parts for the congregation are printed in bold type.

*The congregation will stand.

2

A FESTIVAL OF GREAT HYMNS

Prelude: Prelude and Fugue in F   Dietrich Buxtehude
The Ringing of the Bells
The Lighting of the Candles
Call to Worship

    Minister: Let us worship the Lord.
                (The congregation will stand)
    Minister: O sing to the Lord a new song;
    People: **Sing to the Lord, all the earth!**
    Minister: Declare his glory among the nations,
    People: **His marvelous works among the peoples!**
    Minister: Honor and majesty are before him;
    People: **Strength and beauty are in his sanctuary**

Hymn: Praise to the Lord, the Almighty   Lobe den Herren
    1—U
    2—Ch
    3—U
    4—U

The Bidding Prayer
    (The congregation will remain standing)
        We are met together to do honor to the Lord, to acknowledge with joy
the reign of our Savior Christ, and to pray for the gifts of the Holy Spirit to
be dispersed among us, that we may in spirit sing these praises, make
these offerings, and receive the blessings of God.
        In your prayers give gratitude to God for this company of singers and
players; for the Fort Worth Chapter of the American Guild of Organists, on
its 50th anniversary, founded to promote God's praise; for all the
friendships it has fostered, all the learning it has nourished, and all the
visions it has opened to us.
        Repent before God for the moments of failure, the missed opportunities
and the false ambitions; and remember in his presence, that to him for
whom a thousand years are as yesterday, no sin or failure of which his
children truly repent is ever beyond recovery, and no mistaken journey
ever beyond his power to recall.
        Remember before God all those who having made music on this earth,
now join in the praises of heaven: all composers, performers, and faithful
worshipers who have assisted us to perfect the praise of God in his Church
on earth; those who have been known all over the world, and those who
have no memorial but the comfort they have brought to the people of God
in their own place.
        Remember with compassion all those in whose lives there is no praise;
those upon whom the pressures of life, the unkindness of their fellows, or
their own sin have borne heavily; those who at this time are turned away
from joy by the oppression of anxiety or pain, and commend them all to
the loving heart of the Father.
        And finally, whatever things are honorable, excellent, and worthy of
celebration; whatever things are lovely and gracious and of good report—

3

think on these, and thank God who is the creator of them all.

Praise the Lord. With all your talents and your love, praise him. In the company of angels and archangels and all the choir of heaven, praise him. Let us gather up our prayers and praises in the words which our Lord himself taught us:

Our Father who are in heaven, hallowed be Thy Name. Thy kingdom come, Thy will be done, on earth as it is in heaven. Give us this day our daily bread. Forgive us our debts as we forgive our debtors, and lead us not in temptation, but deliver us from evil. For Thine is the kingdom, and the power, and the glory, for ever. Amen.

God receive our songs, Christ purify our hearts, Holy Spirit empower our hands and our voices. Glory to God on high. **Amen.**

Hymn: Of the Father's Love Begotten   *Divinum mysterium*
    1 — U
    2 — Ch
    3 — U*

A reading from Martin Luther:

We know that music is hateful and intolerable to the evil spirits. And I plainly judge, nor am I ashamed to assert, that there is no art, after theology, that can match music; for it alone, after theology, lends that which otherwise only theology lends, to wit: a quiet and contented mind; a manifest token that the devil, author of baleful cares and of the restlessness of the multitude, flies from the voice of music almost as he flies from the word of theology.

—from a letter to Ludwig Sentl, 1530

Hymn: Jesus, Priceless Treasure   *Jesu, meine Freude*
    1 — U
    2 — O
    3 — H

A reading from Canon Joseph Poole:

Worship without music does not easily soar; and wherever the Church has been concerned to make worship really expressive of truth, music has been used; simple music for the untrained worshipper, more elaborate music for the trained choir. The music of a cathedral choir is the counterpart of the architecture and the stained glass of the building; it is a finely wrought music, in which the musicians offer on behalf of the people what the people would wish to do themselves, if they had the ability.

—from Evenson in Coventry Cathedral, 1970

Anthem: E'en So Lord Jesus, Quickly Come   Paul Manz

Peace be to you and grace from Him
Who freed us from our sins,
Who loved us all and shed His blood
That we might saved be.

Sing Holy, Holy to our Lord,
The Lord, Almighty God,
Who was and is and is to come,
Sing Holy, Holy, Lord!

Rejoice in Heaven, all ye that dwell therein,
Rejoice on earth, ye saints below,
For Christ is coming, is coming soon,
For Christ is coming soon!

E'en so, Lord Jesus, quickly come,
And night shall be no more;
They need no light nor lamp nor sun,
For Christ will be their All!
— Revelation 22 (adapted by Paul Manz)

4

Hymn: God Is Working His Purpose Out   *   *Purpose*
    1 — Ch
    2 — W
    3 — M
    4 — U

A reading from P. T. Forsyth:
> Just as in Christ we see mankind with his sin and woe transfigured to
> goodness, standing through pain, and even through sin, in a height of
> glory not otherwise to be won, deified in a cross and resurrection, and
> there determined as the Son of God with power, so in Art we see, for a
> time at least, mankind and his fate in spiritual and pacifying beauty. Art, in
> this respect, is the echo of religion as the interpreter of life, nature, and
> destiny. Now this, which is more or less achieved by all art, is
> conspicuously accomplished by music. It soothes, transfigures, opens the
> fountains of a greater deep, and bathes us in a world of victory, which
> submerges our griefs so that we see them as lovely as ruined towers at the
> bottom of a clear lake on whose bosom we glide. It has, for the hour, the
> power that faith has for good and all — to unloose, emancipate, and
> redeem. When the ransomed of the Lord return to Zion, it is with singing
> and great joy upon their heads.
>
>   *— from Christ on Parnassus, Chapter 8, 1911*

Hymn: O Sacred Head, Now Wounded   *Passion Chorale*
    1 — Ch
    2 — O
    3 — H

The Thai Dance   P. Wongduen Indravudh, Dancer
> The dancer interprets the text of a Thai hymn, accompanied by harp,
> finger cymbals and tom-tom, as well as her own singing. The texts for the
> two stanzas are:
> Isaiah 55:1
> "Ho, everyone who thirsts,
> Come to the waters;
> And he who has no money,
> Come, buy and eat!
> Come, buy wine and milk
> Without money and without price."
> Matthew 11:28-29
> "Come to me, all who labor and are heavy laden,
> And I will give you rest.
> Take my yoke upon you,
> And learn from me;
> For I am gentle and lowly in heart,
> And you will find rest for your souls."

Hymn: God of Grace and God of Glory   *Cwm Rhondda*
    1 — U
    2 — M
    3 — U
    4 — W
    5 — U

A reading from Joseph Sittler:
> It is here affirmed that there is in nature and history a holy possibility for
> the fulfillment of all things . . . And the comprehensive term for that
> perception and that faith is the glory.
>   Christian worship has always understood this. If one seeks for a word

5

common to the entire spectrum of corporate acknowledgment and adoration, and considers all in that enormous range from calculated Gregorian intervals to the spontaneous outbursts of Appalachian shout and song, from the unearthly shimmer of Palestrina to the rocking rhythms of Negro song — it is the force of the glory that is attested.

. . . When in the nativity stories "the glory of the Lord shone round about," and when the child was greeted as the "glory of thy people Israel," the background is given for the claim that in Christ the glory has concretely come fleshly nigh — "and we beheld his glory, full of grace and truth." And when the darkness of death failed to smother a life luminous with the glory, and the community affirmed him to be alive and creative of nothing less than a new being for men, they put it this way: "Christ was raised from the dead by the *glory* of the Father"!

The glory . . . is the persisting allure that draws and drives all things beyond the vain glory of penultimate meanings. It sings in nerve and blood in D. H. Lawrence, in the arching speculations of Plotinus, and it meets us as a gift, an evocation, and a demand in every dirty street, every hurt upturned face, every failure of fulfillment on the streets of this world.
— from "Epiphany, Glory and 63rd Street"

Hymn: Let All Mortal Flesh Keep Silence   *Picardy*
    1 — Ch
    2 — M
    3 — W
    4 — U

The Receiving of the Offering

A Prayer:
    O God, giver of life and hope and joy, help us to know joy as a spring always welling up within us and giving us the power to dance through life, not as men and women who are blind to sorrow, misery, or shame — but as those who know Your victory over evil and over death and who cannot but rejoice.
    O God of Majesty, whom saints and angels delight to worship in heaven: Be with your servants who make music for your people, that with joy we on earth may glimpse your beauty, and bring us to the fulfillment of that hope of perfection which will be ours as we stand before your unveiled glory. We make this prayer through Jesus Christ our Lord, to whom, with you and the Holy Spirit, be honor and glory through out all ages. Amen.

The Call to the Ushers

The Offertory: Improvisation   Paul Manz

Hymn: For All the Saints   *Sine Nomine*
    1 — U
    2 — M, 2 — U
    3 — U
    4 — Ch
    5 — O
    6 — U*

6

The Church's One Foundation

1. (U) The Church's one foundation
        Is Jesus Christ, her Lord:
        She is His new creation
        By water and the Word.
        From heav'n He came and sought her
        To be His holy bride;
        With His own blood He bought her
        And for her life He died.

2. (Ch) Elect from ev'ry nation,
        Yet one o'er all the earth,
        Her charter of salvation
        One Lord, one faith, one birth.
        One holy name she blesses,
        Partakes one holy food,
        And to one hope she presses,
        With ev'ry grace endued.

3. (U) The Church shall never perish!
        Her dear Lord, to defend,
        To guide, sustain, and cherish,
        Is with her to the end.
        Tho' there be those that hate her,
        False sons within her pale,
        Against both foe and traitor
        She ever shall prevail.

4. (U) Tho' with a scornful wonder
        Men see her sore oppressed,
        By schisms rent asunder,
        By heresies distressed,
        Yet saints their watch are keeping;
        Their cry goes up, "How long?"
        And soon the night of weeping
        Shall be the morn of song.

5. (U) Mid toil and tribulation
        And tumult of her war
        She waits the consummation
        Of peace forever more,
        Till with the vision glorious
        Her longing eyes are blest
        And the great Church victorious
        Shall be the Church at rest.

Benediction

Organ Dismissal: In Thee is Gladness   J. S. Bach
(The congregation will remain seated during the organ dismissal.)

The Ringing of the Bells

7

Bibliography

Arnold, Corliss Richard. *Organ Literature: A Comprehensive Survey.* Vol. I: Historical Survey, Third Edition. Metuchen, N.J., and London: The Scarecrow Press, Inc., 1995.

Brown, Christopher Boyd. *Singing the Gospel: Lutheran Hymns and the Success of the Reformation.* Cambridge, Massachusetts, and London, England: Harvard University Press, 2005.

Earley, Sandra. "Paul Manz: The Hymn Master." *Correspondent* 94, no. 582 (March/April 1996): 7.

Freese, James, ed. *This is the Feast: A Festschrift for Richard Hillert at 80.* St. Louis: MorningStar Music Publishers, 2004.

Gebauer, Victor. "Composers for the Church: Paul Manz." *Church Music* 79, pp. 31-48.

Hymnal 1982, The. New York: The Church Hymnal Corporation, 1982.

Lochner, Martin. *The Organist's Handbook. A Guide to Lutheran Service Playing on Small Pipe-Organ, Reed-Organ, or Piano.* St. Louis: Concordia Publishing House, 1940.

Lutheran Book of Worship. Minneapolis: Augsburg Publishing House, 1978.

Lutheran Hymnal, The. St. Louis: Concordia Publishing House, 1941.

Lutheran Worship. St. Louis: Concordia Publishing House, 1982.

Manz, Paul. "Cantate Domino Canticum Novum – Te Deum: A Life in Church Music" *The Cresset*, September 1993, pp. 7-13.

_____. "Praising God in Words and Music." *Currents in Theology and Mission* 16. June 1989, pp. 169-172.

Schalk, Carl. *Luther on Music: Paradigms of Praise.* St. Louis: Concordia Publishing House, 1988.

_____. *God's Song in a New Land: American Hymnals in America.* St. Louis: Concordia Publishing House, 1995.

Tietjen, John H. *Memoirs in Exile: Confessional Hope and Institutional Conflict.* Minneapolis: Fortress Press, 1990.

Thomashower, James E. "Notable Organists of the Twentieth Century." *The American Organist* 34 (March 2000): 54.

Vajda, Jaroslav J. *So Much to Sing About.* St. Louis: MorningStar Music Publishers, 1991.

With One Voice. Minneapolis: Augsburg Fortress, 1995.

Worship Supplement. St. Louis: Concordia Publishing House, 1969.

Notes

1   For the purposes of this book, a "hymn festival" is a thematic concert of hymns which attempts to bring meaning and insight from the hymns to the participants through musical variations and interpretations by the organist and the musical resources of a church.

2   "Attendance literature" refers to the non-hymn-based organ music often included in a hymn festival.

3   Previous research includes a master's thesis by David Martin Angerman, *The Organ Music of Paul Manz*, (Baylor University, 1982); a doctoral dissertation by Becker Parker Lombard, *A Study of the Life of Paul Otto Manz as a Church Musician, with an Analytical Study of His Organ Compositions*, (New Orleans Baptist Theological Seminary, 1991); and a doctoral dissertation by Scott M. Hyslop, *The Journey Was Chosen: The Life and Work of Paul Manz*, (University of Michigan) published by MorningStar Music Publishers in 2007).

4   Carl F. Schalk. *Luther on Music: Paradigms of Praise.* (St. Louis: Concordia Publishing House, 1988), 13.

5   Christopher Boyd Brown. *Singing the Gospel: Lutheran Hymns and the Success of the Reformation.* (Cambridge, Massachusetts, and London, England: Harvard University Press), 13.

6   Victor Gebauer."Composers for the Church: Paul Manz." *Church Music 79: An Annual Publication of Church Music in America.*" (1979): 33.

7   Ibid., 34.

8   Ibid., 31.

9   Paul Manz, interview by the author, Minneapolis, MN, November 9-11, 2005.

10 Manz interview.

11 Manz interview.

12 Paul Manz, "Cantate Domino Canticum Novum—Te Deum: A Life in Church Music." (*The Cresset*: September 1993): 9.

13 *9 Hymn Improvisations*. (St. Louis: MorningStar Music Publishers, 1994), 18.

14 Gebauer, 32.

15 Manz interview.

16 Manz interview.

17 Manz interview.

18 Gebauer, 37.

19 Manz interview.

20 Manz interview.

21 http://www.bw.edu/academics/libraries/bach/_accessed April 18, 2007.

22 Manz archives.

23 "Cantate Domino," 9-10.

24 Manz interview.

25 James Freese, ed. *This Is the Feast: Richard Hillert at 80*. (St. Louis: MorningStar Music Publishers, 2004). Afterword.

26 Manz interview.

27 "Cantate Domino," 10.

28 Manz interview.

29 "Cantate Domino," 10.

30 Corliss Richard Arnold. *Organ Literature: A Comprehensive Survey. Vol. 1 Historical Survey*. (Metuchen, N. J., and London: The Scarecrow Press, Inc.), 230.

31 Manz interview.

32 Manz interview.

33 Manz interview.

34 Manz interview.

35 Manz interview.

36 Manz interview

37 "Cantate Domino," 10.

38 Arnold, 212.

39 Helmut Walcha, *Chorale Preludes*, Vol. II, p. 60. Translation by Paul Jordan.

40 Manz interview.

41 Manz interview.

42 Manz interview.

43 Manz interview.

44 Manz interview.

45 Manz interview.

46 Manz interview.

47 Walter A. Armbruster. *A Bag of Noodles*. (St. Louis: Concordia Publishing House, 1972).

48 Manz interview.

49 Martin Marty. *A Hymn Festival Celebrating the Lutheran Chorale*, performed by Paul Manz and the Valparaiso University Chorale. Congregational Song Series, number 4. Association of Lutheran Church Musicians, (CD), 2000.

50 *Lutheran Book of Worship*, (Minneapolis: Augsburg, 1978) Hymn 325, stanza 3.

51 Poor quality of the original made it unable to be copied. A transcription of the pertinent part comprises this appendix.

52 Thomas Gieschen, ed. *The Parish Organist*, Vol. 9. (St. Louis: Concordia Publishing House, 1962).

53 Manz interview.

54 Manz interview.

55 Manz interview.

56 Manz interview.

57 Manz interview.

58 Manz interview.

59 Carl Schalk. *God's Song in a New Land*. (St. Louis: Concordia Publishing House, 1995), 14.

60 Ibid., 15.

61 Ibid., 173.

62 Ibid., 173.

63 Ibid., 173-174.

64 Schalk, 175.

65 Ibid., 177.

66 John Tietjen. *Memoirs in Exile: Confessional Hope and Institutional Conflict*. (Minneapolis: Fortress Press), 211-212.

67 Ibid., 212.

68 Ibid., 254.

69 "Cantate Domino," 9.

70 Tietjen, 320-321.

71 Tietjen, 326.

72 Tietjen, 318-319

73 Ibid., 319.

74 Ibid., 319-320.

75 "Tomorrow Shall Be My Dancing Day," traditional English carol, adapted by John Gardner (1933-1982). http://en.wikipedia.org/wiki/Tomorrow_shall_be_my_dancing_day, accessed May 15,2007.

76 Jaroslav J. Vajda. *So Much to Sing About*. (St. Louis: MorningStar Music Publishers, 1991), 88-89.

77 Tietjen, 192.

78 Though he had no sight line to the author, he made a point of saying after the hymn festival, "You read very well." Such was his awareness.

79 James E. Thomashower. "Notable Organists of the Twentieth Century." *The American Organist* 34, no. 3 (March 2000): 54.

80 Kussrow was on the faculty at Valparaiso and was present for the 1963 Liturgical Institute when Manz played his partita on ST. ANNE.

81 Personal correspondence with Mary Bode, April 2007.

82 http://www.bartleby.com/101/318.html, accessed May 17, 2007.

83 Manz interview.

84 Manz interview.

85 *Lutheran Worship*, (St. Louis: Concordia Publishing House, 1982), 243.

86 Robin Leaver. *The Theological Character of Music in Worship*. Church Music Pamphlet Series. (St. Louis: Concordia, 1989), 15.

87 Carl F. Schalk. *Luther on Music: Paradigms of Praise*. (St. Louis: Concordia Publishing House, 1988), 54-55.

88 Paul Manz. "Praising God in Words and Music." *Currents in Theology and Mission* 16. June 1989):170, 171.

89 Ibid.

90 Ibid.

91 Ibid.

92 *Lutheran Worship*, 243.